Finding Awareness

Finding Awareness

The
Journey
of
Self-discovery

Amit Pagedar

Finding Awareness: A Journey of Self-Discovery
Copyright © 2021 Amit Pagedar

Cover Design by C.S. Fritz for Albatross Book Co.
Formatting by Albatross Book Co.

All rights reserved under the Pan-American and International Copyright Convention. This book may not be reproduced in whole or in part, except for the brief quotations embodied in critical articles or reviews, in any form or by any means, electronic or mechanical, including photocopying, recording, or by any information storage and retrieval system now known or hereinafter invented, without permission of the author.

ISBN: 9798721905094

*Arvin, when you're old enough to understand,
I want you to know that I wrote this book for you.*

Contents

Introduction 1

Part 1 - The Way of Suffering
    1 - Who Are We? 9
    2 - Comparison 17
    3 - Unfairness 23
    4 - Insecurity 29
    5 - Self-expression and Connection 33
    6 - Isolation, Anxiety and Stress 39
    7 - Addictive Behaviors 47
    8 - The Blind Retriever 53
    9 - Fear 61
    10 - The Violence Within 71
    11 - Hurt Cycles – Guilt and Regret 77
    12 - The Structure of Suffering 83

Part 2 - Finding Awareness
    13 - Self-awareness 93
    14 - Finding the Bridge 97

15 - Walking the Bridge 103
  16 - The Art of Listening 107
  17 - The Art of Feeling 117
  18 - The Art of Seeing 123
  19 - The Art of Observing 131

Part 3 - Structure of the Ego
  20 - Labels and Judgments 149
  21 - Beliefs 155
  22 - Attachments 165
  23 - The Three Selves 175
  24 - The One Self 183
  25 - Structure of the Ego and the Feeling of Me 189

Part 4 - The Struggle
  26 - Presence and Planning 201
  27 - The Backwards Law 211

Part 5 - Surrender
  28 - The Precipice 223
  29 - Surrender 229

Questions and Answers
  Self-Awareness 235
  Self-Acceptance 249
  Relationships 257
  Meditation 266
  Surrender 275
  Ego 282
  Goals 291

Endnote References 296

Introduction

If you are reading this book, it is possible that you are familiar with my work on Instagram. If not, I hope that you find the contents of this book valuable. Over these past few years, I have had the privilege of speaking with thousands of my readers over hundreds of hours. Many of them shared personal stories and experiences with me as we discussed a wide range of topics. Those conversations were at times emotional and intense. This book is an expansion of the ideas we discussed and the insights we had during those talks. Therefore, I don't own this book anymore than the air I breathe. It belongs to you.

Even though I started sharing my thoughts in 2018 on Instagram under the name @findingawareness, I had been writing for 17 years before then in some form. Though, for all those years whatever I wrote always seemed conceptual or derivative in nature. It came with a peculiar feeling that those ideas weren't authentic. They seemed to be more of an intellectual analysis than pointing to a direct experience. This was further established when I observed my responses to the problems that arose in my life. The conceptual understanding I had amassed was useless. The egoic patterns remained strong. Though superficial changes were

Finding Awareness

happening, the core of me was still the same. It appeared that I was writing from secondhand experiences of those whose ideas filled my mind.

My perspective changed one evening, a little more than two years ago. It was one of those days when I was grappling with emotional upheaval, confusion, and fear. There were many unresolved questions about my past and my future. They had all come looking for answers, and I had nothing to offer. A deep confusion and a sense of profound meaninglessness about my life had taken over. I had been to such a place multiple times before, and every time, some temporary measure had come to my rescue. Either a new book or some new meditation would appear and help me escape my dread and helplessness. Though this time, it felt as if I had nowhere to run. The inner resistance and battle with my own fears and anxieties had come to a head.

That day, about 30 minutes into a meditation session, I began to have an intense headache. The struggle had never been so difficult so as to cause any physical pain before, but there it was. It felt like an obstruction, a psychological barrier which was both intolerable, yet unsurpassable. The rising pressure slowly became impossible to bear. It culminated into a breaking of something I could not name. With it came a wordless feeling of an ending, a washing away of dark shadows from the depths of my being. All movement ceased. There was nothing to hold on to. The mind plunged into the depths of silence. It forgot its own existence. The body became light as a feather. It felt as if the burdens of a thousand lifetimes were lifted. There was a sense of profound bliss.

I had no idea what had taken place nor did I care. All that mattered was my behavior and thinking had undergone an overnight change. The heaviness of the past had left. It felt like a new life was given to me, and there was no point in questioning it. I just wanted to live it. There was no desire to analyze anything. All my hurts, fears, and ambitions felt insignificant. They were there; yet their presence didn't matter anymore. It felt as if I could fail at anything or succeed at anything and it was all the same. There was no fear or anticipation of any pleasure. There was no resistance to anything. The mind was in a state of deep rest.

Though I could tell a positive thought apart from a negative one, there was no emotional reaction to either of them. The words *positive* and the *negative* virtually had lost all their meaning. The darkest thought no longer felt any different than the holiest thought. The battle of opposites was over. All anxiety, confusion and the frustration now seemed like a distant memory. The mind felt effortlessly clear yet sharp. It was sensitive to everything that happened around it, but had no intention of commenting on it, let alone change it. It was immersed, yet somehow, untouched. It didn't matter to me as to why any of this was happening. I simply carried on living in this new way.

Over the next few weeks, I felt a surge of inspiration and started sharing my thoughts on Instagram. As the words started to flow, more people began to resonate with them. One of my readers asked me if I had known of author Eckhart Tolle. I looked at his books sitting on my bookshelf. I had read Eckhart's teachings more than a decade ago. As my memory stretched back in time, a word from one of his books resurfaced and drew me towards it. That word was *surrender*. I had struggled to understand what he had meant all those years ago. I even believed it to be a form of accepting defeat when I had first read his books. Yet now, the same word seemed so obvious and natural. It was here, at the center of my being.

As I continued sharing my ideas, this experience of surrender became a central theme of my writings. I also began to realize how impossible it was to ask someone to do it, and expect them to succeed. It was like asking someone to jump off a mountain with a parachute, before they had seen or climbed the mountain. It was not the starting point at all, and hence couldn't be applied as a solution. There had to be another way.

Finding Awareness

As I thought more about this, it became clear why this deep transformation we seek remains beyond our reach despite our best efforts. We wait for it to come from outside of us. We want others to give it to us. Unfortunately, real self-transformation defies teaching. It makes all teachers ultimately irrelevant. For its nature is to be grown, like a plant. It wants to arise spontaneously. Only then is it real.

Another reason why it's so elusive is because the whole picture is never clear to us. We can solve part of the puzzle here and there, but we don't quite grasp how all the pieces fit together. We look at one source to understand our fears, another for pleasures, and yet another for our ego. These disparate sources become confusing and prevent a total insight into the nature of our being. We see the head, the tail, or the leg of the beast, but never the whole thing. This is why I decided to write this book, to speak about all the aspects of inner lives and explore the connections between them. For unless we see how they fit together, we can't make sense of the whole picture and bring about that spontaneous insight we await.

Think of this book as a seed you can plant in your subconscious mind, which is your garden. If it takes root, it will begin to grow as per the conditions it finds itself in. Sometimes it will grow fast; at other times, it will sprout slowly, yet it will always belong to you. If there is one message I have through this book, it is this: Self-transformation is ultimately a journey that requires time, patience, and care. It is an unraveling of who we *want to be*, and finding our way back to who we *already are*.

Our goal with this book is to undertake a deep meditation, and as such, it won't be an easy ride. We will ask difficult questions and refuse easy answers. We will descend inward step-by-step, together, both shattering and rebuilding our egos many times over. We will disintegrate the old structures until something new is born. In this book, we will explore without any urge to arrive at any conclusion. We shall walk the path of honest self-inquiry with nothing but the light of reason in our hands. Let's see where this journey takes us. Let us begin this meditation into ourselves.

Part 1

The Way of Suffering

1
Who Are We?

We are whoever the world teaches us to be.

A distant cousin of my father was an intimidating figure, both in his physicality and accomplishment. He was the most educated man in my extended family, with three PhDs, and a successful business to his name. Everyone respected him, although I feared him more than anything else. At age 15, any figure of authority speaking with a loud booming voice would worry me. This fear had only amplified after my dad told me, why my uncle was making this surprise visit.

"*Listen to what your uncle says. He wants to talk to you. Take him seriously if you want to make something out of life in the future,*" he admonished me. I had not shown any real interest or promise in my studies, as such, I braced for this intervention. This was a routine in my household. When I struggled with my studies, my parents would invite someone over to talk some sense into me. I knew what to expect. I was prepared, although a little unnerved. Soon he arrived and my mother offered him some tea. After taking a few sips and exchanging pleasantries, he turned to me.

"*I am not here to talk about your studies or education, even though I'm sure your parents would want me to talk about those things,*" he said in a calm tone. *"I am not concerned about those things,"* he said with a dismissive gesture of his hand.

I wondered what was on his mind. The change of plans was unexpected, but I looked forward to hearing about anything but schoolwork. He had my full attention.

"I am here to ask you a question, perhaps the most important question, anyone will ever ask you," he continued. *"I think you are now old enough to understand this. If not, we will find out anyway. So tell me Amit, 'Who are you?'"*

Nobody had seen this coming. My father was as surprised as I was. Silence filled the room.

His question confused me. Who was I, indeed? I thought about it carefully, and then spoke. I didn't want to say anything obvious, so I put together an answer I felt would impress him.

"I am someone who enjoys watching movies, excels at playing video games, and is interested in studying astronomy."

"A good enough answer. Now tell me Amit, do any of your friends like these things too?" he asked.

I replied, *"Yes, they do!"*

"How Interesting. So would you be doing any of those things, had it not been for your friends?", he asked while taking a sip from his tea.

Again, the same silence.

I took a minute to think about it. The more I thought about it, the more it seemed as if everything I liked somehow reflected the things my best friends were doing at the time. I watched the same movies as they did; I was playing the same games, listening to the same music. I even seemed to like astronomy because Carl Sagan's *Cosmos* was popular then, and those who watched it were considered to be smart. It suddenly dawned on me that I was more interested in appearing smart, without any real curiosity in astronomy.

I began to feel uneasy as these reflections flashed over me. My confidence was replaced by self-doubt, yet I wanted to be honest. His tone and demeanor were intent, yet disarming. I could feel genuine concern for me in his voice.

I replied, *"No.. I wouldn't perhaps enjoy any of those things… if it wasn't for my friends."*

"Who are you, if not for your friends and family? Do you know that?", he pressured me.

A mild shock came over me, as he was making me confront the fact that I didn't have any interests of my own. I studied the way my friends did; I read the books that they did; my hobbies seemed to be a reflection of their interests. I had nothing original in that 15-year-old brain of mine. It was an unsettling feeling, which is probably why I still remember that conversation. So I told him the truth.

I said, *"I guess I don't know who I am. I have no idea if I have to be honest."*

"Good. That's the answer I was looking for. At least you are honest," he continued. *"You don't get too far ahead if you emulate others. Most people won't admit that whatever occupies their mind is put there by someone else. Remember, what you study is not important, if you are doing it to please your parents. None of it matters if you don't learn how to think for yourself. Even if you go wrong following your own instincts, that's okay, for your regrets will still be your own. If you go astray following someone else, then you don't own even your regrets! That's a terrible place to be as an adult. Do you understand me? This is all I have to say to you."*

This conversation was my first experience with self-awareness. I reflected on it as I began to ponder the question of how we think about ourselves. If we are to begin this journey of self-knowing, we have to

Finding Awareness

examine how it all began. Let's see if we can approach this concept of self-knowledge, as directly as possible.

When someone asks us, *"Who are you?,"* what do we usually say? We tell them our name, our profession, perhaps our nationality, and various other things that describe us. This is our identification. It consists of facts and information about us. Although that doesn't really say who we are, does it? Who *are* we beyond these facts and information? How do we understand and relate to *ourselves*?

Our early self-knowledge begins not with knowing ourselves at all, but by knowing our parents. As children we didn't have a sense of self, let alone self-knowledge. All we knew was that there were these two individuals who cared for us. We didn't have any concept of the world or reality beyond what these two people were doing. When they smiled, we smiled. When they put their tongue out, we did the same. Those were our first experiences.

As my three year old son watches me type on the keyboard, he wants to jump in my lap and do the same. When I walk my dog, my son wants to hold the leash, just the way I do. When his mother is practicing yoga, he lays on his back and touches his toes. All he wants to do is emulate the people around him. He is watching and learning, not just about the world, but about himself too.

When we are young, our entire world revolves around our parents. When they praise us, we know we did something right. When they correct us, we realize we did something wrong. The only way we can distinguish right from wrong is through their feedback. We have no references of our own, no system to discern right from wrong. We have no rational thinking ability or any framework for decision-making. To us, whatever feels right seems right, and whatever feels wrong seems wrong. That's why chocolate is right, and vegetables are wrong. This continues until our caregivers tell us otherwise.

The first definitions of right or wrong are therefore never our own, they are given to us by our caregivers. These definitions form the basis of how we relate to the world. When we enter adolescence, our relation-ship with our parents has already formed a baseline of our self-knowledge. During this age, some parents don't want their children to ever be hurt as they explore the world around them, and therefore overprotect them, which was the case with my parents. On the other hand, some parents have never known adequate protections as children themselves, so they (often unknowingly) under-protect their children. They let their children falter too often, resulting in fearful and anxious core experiences. This, unfortunately, describes the majority of us. Let's look at both these cases and how they relate to our self-knowledge.

If we were overprotected, our parents controlled the smallest of our decisions. Our question, *"What should I do now?"* almost never went unanswered. They decided what we should eat, wear, read, think, whom we were allowed to play with and so on. They overbearingly shaped and reshaped our definitions of right and wrong as we were entering young adulthood. They shielded us from every problem, protected us from all harm, and, in doing so, made us deeply dependent on them.

On the other hand, those of us who were under-protected as children took a much more treacherous path. Our parents constantly fought with each other and ignored our basic needs. In some cases, they separated, creating deep trauma and confusion in our lives. They made us choose between them. They lamented about their relationship issues as if we knew the answers that they didn't. We were only children. To us, those were impossible problems to solve. This constant barrage of difficult problems, and the inability to solve them, took a toll on our self-esteem and self-confidence. There was no safe space for our minds to go when it needed protection. We began to see ourselves as afraid and insecure.

In both cases, whether we were insecure, or dependent we had to eventually face society in some form. First it was our peers in high-school,

Finding Awareness

then our college and then perhaps our first job. Each time we made a foray into an alien world, whose rules we barely understood. We didn't know how to be in this new world. We approached it either with over-confidence (a result of inexperience in solving our own problems) or deep insecurity (a result of having faced unsolvable problems). When our expectations crashed with reality, we made mistakes—we didn't fit in. We were emotionally too timid or too defiant. Up until then, we didn't need new people in our lives. But now we were thrust in the middle of them, and they didn't seem to agree with us on anything. It began to dawn on us that if we must fit into this new society, we must somehow get its approval. We must ask it to teach us right from wrong.

Each time our social exposure widens and we enter high-school, college, graduate school or work, we go back to being children again – looking up to the new world to teach us its ways. As children, our parents were our guiding lights. Now, our friends have to pick up the mantle. We ask this new world, *"What should I do now?"*, just like we did when we were small children. We ask our friends to show us how to speak, how to act, how to dress and what to eat, so that they may accept us. This is the state I was in when my uncle introduced me to self-awareness. I was looking to my friends to know how I should be.

In this new society, instead of a pat on the back, we look for that compliment on the way we look. Instead of a *"no,"* we look for hidden cues as to what's cool and what's out. We begin to rely on this new parent to tell us how we should be. Naturally, once we ask this society how to be, we give it control over us. We start moving away from our unique nature and be cast in the mold they have cut out for us. We begin to conform and shape ourselves in their image. In other words, we become whoever the world tells us we should be. There is no point in trying anything different. We better fall in line, for unless we do, we may not be deemed worthy of their acceptance. We may become 'orphans' without the acceptance of this new caregiver.

This is how the *curse of comparison* first enters our lives – with a promise of acceptance and through it, some self-knowledge. Some of us have grown up while being compared to our siblings by our parents, or other kids at school by our teachers. Yet, when we are trying to find our place in a new social dynamic, comparison with others takes on a whole different meaning. We want to desperately find out who we are and comparison offers all the easy answers. We become eager to take on whatever identity the world is ready to give us, as long as it leads to some form of acceptance and security. As long as we are *seen*, we are willing to follow.

So who we are, is essentially a sum total of the people the world has taught us to be. We are whoever the world has taught us to be. We have emulated and patterned ourselves after others through this comparison for decades. Comparison has always provided the reference point by which we found our place in the world. This tendency becomes entrenched over a period of years.

It gives us this incurable habit of comparing ourselves the instant we feel uncertain about our path.

We certainly had an opportunity to reject this way of being and learn who we really were. But unfortunately, we took the path of least resistance to self-knowledge, and here we are. Perhaps this is one of the main reasons why most of us feel as if we are still wandering. We are still walking down that wrong turn we made all those years ago. We were so desperate to find ourselves, that we walked down a lane some stranger pointed to, and never looked back.

2
Comparison

To compare is to let someone else decide our self-worth.

We saw in the previous chapter how comparison presented itself as an easy way to acquire self-knowledge in our past. Let's examine this phenomena in detail. It seems quite intuitive to look at what others are doing in order to judge the merits of our own actions. For instance, we question whether we are earning enough money after looking at how much our friends are earning. If it's comparable, we are satisfied. If not, we feel insecure. If we have a different set of friends who don't earn as much as we do, we feel secure among them. Our friends are merely an arbitrary set of people we have associated with. Yet, because of our tendency to compare, we make them a reference point to evaluate our self-worth. Such comparison and competition may create an unnecessary dissatisfaction with our standard of living.

     Does that mean there's something inherently wrong with comparison? Why can't we shake this habit of comparing ourselves? Why does it feel so natural to compare in spite of the suffering it creates?

Finding Awareness

What is comparison at its root? Simply put, it is to hold two or more things side by side and *measure* them, right? We compare and measure anything we are trying to understand. Without measuring something we can't understand it. If we can't understand something, how can we hope to change it? The core reason why we measure anything is to be able to change it, eventually. Measurement always serves a purpose – to gain control over some aspect of our lives.

Primitive humans needed to measure the length, thickness, flexibility, aerodynamics of their arrows, bows or spears for maximum efficiency. If they had to climb a tree using a rope, they had to measure the length of the rope *compared* to the height of the tree. If they needed to get back to their families before sunset, they had to *compare* the duration of each sunset with the time it took to walk home. Measurement was required for every aspect of human survival. Without comparison and measurement, we would have no technology, no medicine, no agriculture, no space travel – nothing. Humanity wouldn't have survived.

Our entire scientific endeavor originates broadly from two primary desires: our curiosity to learn about our universe and our desire to change the environment to suit our needs. The word *science* itself comes from an old Latin word *scire*, which means *to know*. Science is the pursuit of knowledge and the understanding of our natural world – both of which are acquired through measurement - the basis of all comparison. For all scientific inquiry, comparison and measurement are essential.

Accordingly, comparison appears to be indispensable to the *outer or physical* aspect of human lives, for without it our modern lives would be impossible. However, what importance do comparison and measurement have in our inner lives? We use them both in our personal lives too, don't we? We want to know if we are happier, smarter, richer, better looking, or more popular or successful than others. We compare material possessions like the size of a house, or value of the car we drive. Not only that, but we even compare our egos and our level of spiritual understanding too.

Objective scales exist in the outer world. We can measure something in feet, in pounds, or in ounces. But can we measure the weight of our thoughts or the depth of our emotions? Can we measure love? Can we accurately measure fear or suffering? In the inner world, there are no scales, no standards, no thresholds, no baselines, or references. When our tendency to compare, moves from the physical world to the psychological world, from outer to the inner, it goes from being accurate to being inaccurate, from objective to being subjective, from scientific to being unscientific, from real to being imaginary, and from meaningful to meaningless.

Measuring the monetary value of the car we drive has meaning in the external world, for if we sell the car we get back its worth in some way. But in the inner world measuring our self-worth because of that car has no meaning at all. Yet, that is how some of us define our self-worth. If it's not a car then it's something else: how important our job is; what our reputation is; how successful our careers are; how many hours we can meditate; or who we are married to. It's all the same. We are comparing where comparison has no utility or meaning.

The moment we contrast our inner life with someone else's, we begin to feel conflicted. If we compare 'down,' we create contempt or pity for those who we think are worse. If we compare 'up,' we create insecurity and fear in ourselves. We were subconsciously hoping to find control, instead, we only lost control over our state of mind. We were hoping to learn and know ourselves, yet we only sowed more confusion.

The tendency to compare in the inner world may have had some merit if we were able to compare every single aspect of our lives with that of someone else. For instance, there is no use comparing our wealth with someone else's, unless we also compare how many hours of work we are each putting in to create it. Then we would have to see who was more efficient. However, that may not be enough either. What about the richness of personal experience? Who then, is living their purpose, and who

Finding Awareness

is simply toiling away? What about who had better opportunities, better luck or privileges to begin with that helped them along the way?

Now, let's assume for a moment that we were able to forge ahead and keep comparing our inner lives on these lines. Then the question arises, how long and how many times are we supposed to perform this exercise? At which point is our answer satisfactory? The process of comparison is endless, and therefore it is always incomplete. No matter how much we compare our inner lives with those of others, we can never find the answers we are looking for. That's because we can never know ourselves fully through comparison. We can only know ourselves, *as compared with someone else, which isn't self-knowing at all.* It's kind of like remembering the location of where you parked your car, based on its distance from other cars parked around it. If those other cars move, you'll never find your car! Or knowing the location of a city on a map based on its distance from other cities. We'll never get there, for how do we find those cities without knowing how they relate to the ones near them?

When we compare ourselves with the people around us, our identity, the way we see ourselves, becomes entangled with theirs. Those of us who grew up with the same set of friends know this well. When someone in that circle starts a successful business, or writes a book, or wins some award, it makes everyone else insecure. If they get a job that makes them rich, it makes everyone else feel poor! This is because comparison ensures that we know the ground beneath our feet, based on the ground under someone else's.

> *If they move, we don't know where we stand, and that makes us panic.*

Upon recognizing this, some of us believe that the only person we ought to compare ourselves with, is *our past self*. That seems fair, doesn't it? We set our own standards, our own goals, and keep comparing with our past versions as to whether we reached them. This belief indicates the depth at which comparison has seeped into our psyche. We can't live without comparing and competing. We think, *"If not others, let me at least compete with myself and feel better about my progress"* or *"How will I know how far I have come, if I don't compare with a past version of myself?"* Let's examine these reasons a little more closely.

The first thing we have to do is acknowledge the fact that we are sustaining the habit of comparing. We are unable to let go of it, so we modify it slightly. If we are engaging in the habit anyway, what is stopping our mind from switching back to comparing with *someone else*? Our discipline and will-power? If we had such will-power wouldn't we have overthrown this habit out entirely? Instead we watered it down and kept it around. So comparing with a past version of ourselves, is still plain old comparison. In fact, it is an acknowledgement of our powerlessness in the face of this entrenched habit.

Secondly, how does one *not* know that they have progressed? Whether we are speaking of our career, our skill in yoga, music or in business, when there is progress, we know it instantly. We feel elated when we get a raise at work or when we are able to hold a difficult pose in yoga, play a complex composition or sign a new contract. We were able to undertake and complete a harder task than we could before. When we make progress we always discover it in *real time*. We rarely discover it by comparing our present state with a past version of ourselves. That comparison happens only *afterwards* when we have a desire to congratulate ourselves on our accomplishments. We look back and think, *"I have come so far,"* and then pat our backs. Comparing ourselves with our past selves serves no purpose either. Then why do we do it?

We do it because we are afraid to fall behind. We want to compete and since *outright comparison is frowned upon*, we switch to a more secretive way of comparing with our past self. Our fundamental goal, to get ahead in life, never changed. *So fear seems to be at the root of all our comparison.* We will deal with fear later in the book in more detail.

So if we proceed carefully and honestly, we discover the absurdity of comparison and become free of it on all levels. Once comparison stops making sense, it gradually falls away on its own.

However, comparison does have one, let's call it, *virtue*. It reveals an underlying principle of life which many of us struggle with: that some of us have a different starting point than others. Some of us have innumerable systemic advantages such as wealth, privilege, race or class while others have insurmountable obstacles such as deprivation, disability or chronic illnesses. Some of us have everything given to us on a platter and others have to struggle desperately just to have two meals a day.

Comparison reveals the role that unfairness and luck play in our lives. This reality of unfairness has to be deeply understood if we want to have any deep insight into ourselves. For without understanding unfairness, we may never be able to look at our own lives without the profound pain that unfairness creates. Every explanation and insight we have could be diluted by our inability to understand how unfairness factors into it. Let's see if we can examine and understand it in the next chapter, for to look at the unfairness of life with an open mind is one of the hardest things to do.

3
Unfairness

Life isn't fair or unfair, it just is.

As I am writing this, my son, who is three years old, is playing with our eight-year-old collie-shepherd mix. Even though they both love each other, they also compete with each other for their parents' love. My son pushes my dog away when he wants all the attention, and my dog wiggles his way between me and my son if given a chance. My dog seems to think that it's not fair to him that after five years of getting all the love and attention, a tiny human became the top priority in the household. My son seems to think the same way. So my role as a parent is to teach both of them to treat each other with kindness and respect, for if they do so, then their relationship can develop into a bond.

There is an underlying assumption here, that their kindness and respect towards each other will always be responded in kind. This is the expectation of fairness. We teach our children to practice cooperation and altruism in all their relationships hoping that the society will reciprocate. We teach them to work hard such that their efforts will bear fruit one day. This is the basic concept of fairness that is programmed in our psyche. It creates predictability and security in our relationships and in our life. It's power lies in a simple idea – *if I keep doing my work, I will be rewarded*. This expectation forms the rationale for all our life's work, at personal, inter-personal or at social levels. Our society functions because of this implicit assumption of reciprocal fairness, not just from people, but from life itself.

Research done on non-human primates shows that this expectation of fairness runs far deeper than we tend to think. When an experimenter gives a better reward to one primate for doing the same task compared to the other, the other will express anger and even refusal to participate in the experiment. It is almost as if the animal is saying, *"Why does he get two bananas and I get only one for doing the same thing? This isn't fair!"* So if this desire to expect fairness from life is so fundamental to us, why does fairness often seem like a rare commodity not just in human society, but also in life? Let's look at both.

This is so because we prioritize fairness *from* others, not necessarily to them. Our selfishness gets in the way. The result can be seen in the society we have created. It aspires to fairness on one hand, but it also rewards selfishness. If greed is rewarded, all it takes is for one person, or a group, to take advantage of everyone who is expecting equity. For instance, if everyone believes in playing a certain game by the rules, the person who cheats always ends up winning. To the rest of the players, this is unjust.

Our expectation of fairness is in direct conflict
with our desire for selfishness.

Though, this isn't just a human quality. This conflict between co-operation and selfishness stems from nature itself. It is observed in multiple species of animals, birds, and even bacteria. Lions, for instance, live in prides where they protect each other from intruders. Yet, when the cubs grow up to be adults and take over other prides, they will not hesitate to kill the cubs in the new pride to establish control and pass on their genes.

Lions, just like humans, are *both co-operative and selfish*. As a result, some lion cubs are lucky, while others aren't.

As long as co-operation and selfishness exist,
so will fairness and injustice.

So where do these opposing tendencies come from? If they are so widespread among all life forms they are perhaps a symptom of nature itself. Maybe the conflicting tendencies for selfishness and fairness evolved as a part of the natural order (or disorder). Nature wasn't taking sides. It was indifferent. So if evolution of life itself has no interest in enforcing fairness, it would mean that fairness is never guaranteed, or perhaps *unfairness* has a role to play too.

This is why luck plays a major role in all our relationships, successes and failures. When luck is against us, we think of life as being unfair and unpredictable. Unpredictability, it seems, is *not a bug, but a feature of this system*. Our plans, in spite of our best intentions, may not matter that much. Even though in hindsight, what we have accomplished seems like an achievement, we perhaps just got lucky!

For instance, we don't consciously control the beating of our hearts, the reliable functioning of our complex immune systems, or even our breathing. These processes are simply unfolding on their own. We can't order our stomachs to digest food, our kidneys to function properly or our bowels to have their timely movements. We don't have any conscious control over even the basic aspects of being alive. Our claim to control seems to be rooted in the fact we can indirectly influence these mechanisms.

For example, we can starve ourselves, or fix a broken bone, or take vaccines to fight viruses. Yet, it's clear that these are indirect methods of influence and we have no direct control over our bodies, apart from being able to move them around. Control, when it comes to the inner workings of our own body, is an illusion. As such, anything could go wrong in this moment, and we would be powerless to stop it. Life is *fundamentally unpredictable* and therefore it evokes a deep and a justified fear that it could be unfair to us.

It appears that this word *unfair* is a convenient label we use to describe life. We compare ourselves with others and conclude our situation to be uneven. However, it may seem so only because life is indifferent to the needs of any individual. Even at the deepest levels of existence, it seems to be taking *no sides whatsoever*. It's simply on its way. This idea sounds depressing to us if we are invested in the idea of a protective consciousness overseeing all of life (otherwise it seems quite liberating).

Some of us have strong religious beliefs that prevent us from viewing the forces of life as being detached from us. We derive great security from believing that there is a power watching over us and it's invested in our individual well-being. Such beliefs, at some level, are quite beneficial. They help us maintain a semblance of security and sanity. However, despite our belief in a god or a universal-consciousness, we find ourselves facing the winds of unpredictability and unfairness. Our beliefs can give some meaning to our suffering, but they bring us no closer to *preventing* it. In other words, suffering finds each one of us one way or another. It doesn't care about what we believe in.

Life is not fair or unfair, it is simply *indifferent*.

Now, we can see all this, and still acknowledge that if we were abused as young children or exploited by someone we trusted, life has been unfair to us. If our loved one passed away, what did we ever do to deserve it? What is the reason why some of us suffer so much? These incidents, large or small, shock our nervous system and leave behind indelible trauma.[1]

---
1   We will not deal with trauma directly in this book since there is already a lot of great work therapists and psychologists have done in this field. As far as this book is concerned, all past painful experiences leave behind varying degrees of trauma on our minds. There are ways we can deal with it, as we will discover along the way.

The process of healing from that trauma then becomes a lifelong journey. Along this path of healing, it's natural to ask oneself, *"Why me?"* and demand an answer.

This suffering, on the surface, feels like it was designed solely for us, as if the hand of providence picked us out specifically to be tormented. It makes us feel isolated. We are blinded by our pain to such a degree that we forget to notice how everyone around us is suffering too. Pain has this strange power to make everyone feel alone and forget that they are anything but. We aren't suffering alone, but as a part of the whole misfortune of mankind; that when we suffer, the whole of humanity suffers with us. Our anguish isn't the isolating, but the unifying factor between us.

This is where we can make some room for gratitude in our life. We can remind ourselves that life is incredibly hard for those with a terminal illness, recovering from devastating accidents, living in abject poverty, or ravaged by disease and wars. To them, having what we would call a *normal day filled with boredom* would feel like a blessing. We all have suffered, but some of us are still a *lot* more fortunate than others. It's easy for us to overlook the relative peace and quiet we experience every day, and even take it for granted.

To be sure, this is not to belittle our own hardships, but an attempt to see that if we all suffer in great or small ways, we are connected to the rest of humanity. It's an attempt to awaken both our gratitude and compassion, for ourselves and the world. If we frequently remind ourselves of the immensity of human suffering it corrects our perspective and brings balance and context to the way we see our personal problems. This keeps our compassion and humanity alive. It keeps our heart open. It brings dignity to our suffering.

If we don't feel this connection with humanity then we are likely to feel far more isolated than we actually are. We may think, *"Life is so unfair to me. I am alone in my suffering. I must protect myself at all costs."*

Finding Awareness

This is how our insecurity is born. It arises out of a feeling of a profound isolation and defensiveness.

In the next chapter, let's look at this insecurity and see where our search leads us.

4
Insecurity

We believe that we protect ourselves because we were hurt, yet, our insecurity ensures that we are hurt because we are protecting ourselves.

In the past few years of talking to my readers, one of the most intractable problems they seemed to face was that of insecurity. It was a major roadblock to their peace of mind, happiness, relationships and even goals. As I spoke to them I realized whenever we discussed insecurity, our conversations veered towards our fears. Insecurity and fear seemed to be one and the same problem. Then we would begin to talk about how to address our fears and forget about insecurity. This, I feel, is the first misconception we ought to clear, if insecurity is to be understood.

One of the reasons why insecurity often lingers for years is because of its similarity to fear. We mistake our insecurity for fear and address it accordingly. We deploy temporary measures, such as avoidance, feigning courage, or holding on to our faith, in the face of our insecurity. Since we don't address the root cause, our insecurity remains. As we will see in the chapter on fear, courage is not the right solution, even for fear, let alone for insecurity.

Finding Awareness

So let's explore what insecurity is and why it is different from fear.

Fear and insecurity often appear together, but they differ in important ways. Fear is an acute phenomenon. It is triggered occasionally, such as the fear of heights, of giving a speech, or of touching insects. As such fears may arise and fade away. Insecurity, however, is more of an under-current. It remains. We generally don't wake up in the morning afraid, since none of our fears are yet active. Although, we may certainly wake up feeling insecure. Fear is being afraid of a specific thing at a particular time. Insecurity is being afraid of *nothing specific, all the time.*

Our fears may not impact our self-esteem. It rarely causes feelings of unworthiness. Insecurity almost always does.

No amount of education or worldly accomplishments can protect us from low self-worth if we suffer from deep-seated insecurity.

We could have everything in the world and still think of ourselves as a fraud. Our fears describe how we relate to the world, but our insecurity describes how we relate to *ourselves*. Fear makes us feel unsafe out there. Insecurity makes us feel unsafe *in here*, within our own bodies. If we don't feel safe in our own home, we act as if we are under some kind of an unknown threat, all the time. This worry manifests in all our relationships.

If we are insecure, it's possible to feel threatened in a relationship even if our partner is nothing but loving and supportive. Our insecurity tries to protect us from a past hurt or trauma from recurring, regardless of its likelihood. It ignores the evidence in front of its eyes, but values the evidence from it's past. It could be that a parent abandoned us, or a partner mistreated us a long time ago. Perhaps we suffered sexual abuse as children or adults. Given these traumatic events, it's natural to feel anxious about being intimate even with a loving partner. The more harrowing our experience, the deeper our present insecurity. All our mental resources get employed in preventing that trauma from recurring. Everything else becomes secondary.

Insecurity therefore becomes a vicious cycle. We believe that we are protecting ourselves because we were hurt (which is true), yet it ensures that we continue to get hurt for the very same reason. Why does this happen?

Insecurity makes us paranoid. It constantly says, *"What if I get hurt again? I must stay vigilant and protect myself at all costs."* It creates a hesitation in the way we think, speak and act. When there is self-doubt in our speech, those who we speak to, perceive it and begin to hedge as well. They think, *"Why is she hesitating? Is she hiding something? She doesn't trust me."* Insecurity is the lack of trust with oneself, but it manifests as a lack of trust with others. When we act insecure, we make others feel as if we are doubting their intentions.

> Our perceived lack of trust pushes them away.

Because of the constant threat, insecurity prevents us from listening deeply. We can't connect with our partner. Over a period of time, they can't connect with us either. It creates a deep chasm in our relationships. When neither of us wants to overcome it, it's only a matter of time before one of us accidentally offends the other. Since we have stopped listening to each other's emotional needs, a misunderstanding is inevitable. Frequent misunderstandings are a hallmark of insecure relationships. We protect ourselves because we were hurt, and now we receive hurt because we are protecting ourselves. The hurt cycle restarts.

Imagine if you were a guard on a watchtower, and your only job was to send out of a signal if you saw any threats on the horizon. There's daylight and you have a pair of binoculars you can use to keep an eye out. If there were no threats around you, you would stand down, right? What if it was dark, and you couldn't see anything? Then you would never stand down. You'd always be on high alert. Insecurity turns us into that nightwatchman. That's why we are always in an anxious state of mind, for a threat could come from anywhere.

Insecurity, much like this darkness, makes us focus only on self-protection. We have no time or mental space left for self-reflection. That's why insecurity never leaves. Its purpose is to keep us hyper-vigilant. Its nature is to prevent us from observing, knowing and understanding ourselves and dispelling the darkness within. Just as darkness is the absence of light, and has no existence of its own, neither does insecurity. It is simply an absence of security.

You don't have to fight darkness, you only have to bring in light. If we fight this darkness it can consume us. So we work on our insecurity just by leaving it alone, and walking down the path that leads to security. If insecurity is sustained only through our inability to look within, then security would naturally arise if we did the opposite. If the inability to look within extends the dark night of insecurity, then the rise of self-awareness must be the light that ends it.

> NOTE:
> In the next chapter, we will see how our insecurity not only creates a hindrance to looking inward, but also becomes the primary source of unhappiness in our lives. We will see how insecurity manifests in our life and slowly pushes us towards emotional isolation, stress and darker problems. On the road that we are on, we are still far away from finding any permanent solutions to insecurity. We are only beginning our descent, inwards.

5
Self-expression and Connection

When we realize that we are unable to express ourselves, we avoid facing not just other people, but even ourselves.

Imagine you're on a train ride during a vacation in a scenic country. You're sitting by the window, admiring the natural beauty of the land. As you are engrossed in this observation, you get a phone call from your best friend. When you tell her where you are, she's delighted and implores you to describe all that you're seeing outside your window. The train is moving fast, yet you try to relay as many things as possible. *"We are passing a small village, there's a meadow with cows grazing. In the far back, I can see some mountains with snow-clad peaks, and now we are approaching a lake. The water is clear and blue."* Your friend isn't satisfied with your lackluster performance. She says, *"You just went through a list of things you saw, but you didn't really give me the details. I want to feel like I am there with you right now. Bring me into your space, paint me a better picture."*

So you start over and describe the sights again. Yet, your friend still isn't satisfied. After a few attempts you feel frustrated and give up. You feel as if you tried your best, yet she didn't want to listen. You are annoyed and upset that she gave you such a hard time. When you reach your hotel room, you put some time aside to ponder what really happened in that conversation. Why did it end up this way?

When you meditate upon it you realize that the train wasn't going slow enough for you to see everything. Otherwise, you could have described the shapes of all the houses you saw in that village, and the neat little gardens in their front yards. You could have described the bright red, the purple, the pink and the blue flowers you saw. You could have told her how the cows had bells around their necks that jingled as they walked or how there was also a sheep-dog guarding them. You could have mentioned that the mountains in the back shimmered as the sun's rays bounced from their snow-clad peaks, and made dancing reflections on the lake. Then perhaps she would have been able to understand you. You had no time to see, and therefore, no means to describe all that you saw.

The train in this narrative is our life, and the scenes outside the window are our thoughts, emotions and feelings. The speed of the train is the velocity of our thoughts. Our mind is always occupied and working, and never still. We, therefore, can't see the contents of our thoughts as well as we would like, and can't express them to anyone. No matter how beautiful our internal world is, we can't let others in. Our ability to communicate is the heart and soul of our connection with our loved ones.

> Perhaps the greatest problem an insecure person faces in their relationships is their inability to express themselves unequivocally.

Self-expression, at its root, is self-description. When an artist paints a picture, she is describing what's inside her mind by putting it on the canvas. In a similar way, we are all artists, illustrating our inner realities, every time we speak. This is why the words we choose reflect our inner states. We can't speak calmly if we are angry. Neither can we shout at someone if we are peaceful. If we are unaware of our inner states, we choose the wrong words to describe them. We are miscommunicating.

As a result, when we have an emotional need, we aren't able to articulate it. We equivocate and approximate what's within. If we need our partner to be with us and listen, we can't put it into words. Instead we express anger or resentment. If we are unable to tell our story, we walk away from every conversation feeling as if our partner (or friend) wasn't listening to us. Whereas, the reality was that we never gave them a chance in the first place. They can, perhaps, play their part of listening, if we can do our part of speaking. But we can't, because our mind is an enigma to us.

It's not our fault though. As we saw in the previous chapter, an insecure mind has only one goal, to protect itself. It is always occupied, battling imaginary threats. It is caught up in a stream of fearful thoughts and emotions. It is in motion, just like a train. Often this train has no brakes, and can't slow down. So when we are conversing, the right time to speak our mind never arises. We are always trying to catch up as we keep missing the window. When we speak, we leave our sentences unfinished, or we cut them short. There is never enough time to express everything that we want to say. So sometimes, we stay quiet altogether.

This is why if we are insecure, we often end up with a myriad of unsaid things in our relationships. We have a lot to say, but we can't. We feel bottled up. This incapacity to communicate soon becomes a part of our self-image. We say, *"I am a poor communicator"* or *"I am unable to have deep meaningful relationships"* or *"I guess I am just an introvert."* We label ourselves as being introverted, recluse, emotionally sensitive, poor communicators, or even insecure, all of which have their roots in something ordinary, such as insufficient self-expression.

These labels are harmful, for they tend to become self-fulfilling prophecies. For instance, if we judge ourselves to be introverts,

Finding Awareness

it rationalizes our inability to communicate. This isn't to say that all introverts are poor communicators, just that sometimes these labels conceal what we don't want to confront. Once we assume that we are introverts or poor communicators, we give up the desire to improve our self-observation and self-expression. What are the consequences of this?

Since we don't need to open up to others, we refuse to be open with ourselves too. We feel, *"Why should I attempt to examine my own feelings, if I am not good at emotionally connecting with others anyway?"* After all, why should one go through the trouble of cleaning up one's house, if one is never allowing visitors? It makes perfect sense to leave things as they are. It makes perfect sense to refuse to look inwards. This is why if we have an insecure partner in our relationship, we have trouble asking them to look at themselves in an objective way. It's not their fault. They simply are unable to.

> This is also why those of us who are insecure find meditation and self-examination impossible.

This creates a deep contradiction in our lives, because human beings aren't made to live this way. We have evolved to live in structured, close-knit family units. We are inclined to seek warmth and comfort through our connections and relationships. Our common ancestors evolved sitting around a bonfire sharing meals, telling stories, laughing together and crying together. They fought together, raised children together, and died together. This is the true human connection we have always been seeking. This core desire to connect is programmed in every cell of our body. It's healthy, sane, and brings balance and happiness to our lives. This is what we wanted in the beginning chapters too, when we looked for acceptance from our friends.

So, when we are unable to look inwards because of our insecurity, we also pull away from our primary social drive to seek deep and meaningful connections. *Insecurity puts us in direct conflict with our innate need for bonding.* This creates a profound emptiness in our lives. We feel as if there is no meaning to anything that we are doing, even though we may have great careers, wealth and comfort. We feel lost because we have moved far away from the greatest source of meaning and happiness – a deep connectedness with other human beings. We soon find ourselves in a state of *emotional isolation.*

> NOTE:
> As we proceed step-by-step inwards, it is apparent that we have not looked at any practical or direct solutions to insecurity. We have gotten only a glimpse of the direction in which the answers lie. This is so because the only permanent solution to our insecurity is self-knowledge. As our self-knowledge grows, our insecurity decreases. There is nothing else to be done about it. As we proceed inwards we realize that the next state to be understood is that of emotional isolation. Let's understand the role it plays in our self-awareness journey.

6
Isolation, Anxiety and Stress

To be emotionally isolated is to be locked in the space of not being understood, while feeling powerless to do anything about it.

Each one of us feels lonely at some point in our lives. Whether we think of ourselves as secure or insecure, most of us have to eventually move away from the comfort of our homes, whether it's for college, a new job or for other reasons. I remember the first day I came into the United States. I had never lived more than an hour away from my home in the warm tropical weather of Mumbai in 21 years. Now, I found myself on the other side of the planet, away from my friends and family, living in Syracuse – a city that routinely had its streets covered with a foot of snow in the winter. I was terrified of being alone.

As time went on, that acute social isolation began to subside. I began to have conversations and build connections that soon developed into meaningful friendships. However, not all of us were so lucky. For some people who came with me, it was a trying time. They grappled with the harsh reality of becoming self-reliant. As time went on, an overwhelming

Finding Awareness

sense of isolation overcame them. It certainly took a heavy toll on one of my friends during that time.

He was not only a brilliant sketch artist but also a sharp student. I spent a lot of time with him discussing books, art, and various other things. Little did I know that I was perhaps the only person he interacted with. As many months passed by and I got to know him better, I realized that despite his artistic talents and his academic brilliance, he always seemed to be fighting an inner battle. One day when we met over coffee, he sat down but wouldn't make eye contact. He looked upset over something.

"What's up?", I asked him.

He said, *"I am leaving."*

"Leaving for where?" I asked, alarmed by the suddenness of this news.

"I am going back home."

This wasn't uncommon among international students studying in the United States. But this was different. He excelled at his schoolwork.

"But you're doing so well. It's been ten months since you have come here. The year is almost up. Why go back now?" I implored.

"You don't understand. I feel too alone here."

"Well, we are all alone here. We just make it work, right?"

"Not all of us. Some of us are more lonely than others. You won't understand. Sorry."

"Well, maybe. Can you help me understand?" I urged him.

"Look, you are perhaps the only friend I have, which is why I came here to tell you. For some reason we got along, but this is quite rare for me. The truth is, I am not able to connect with anyone. I find it very hard to express myself. I have never felt heard or understood."

"What about your classmates? You don't get along with them?"

"I have tried. Some of them have said hurtful things even though I haven't opened up to them. I wonder what they would have done had I been more vulnerable with them. But none of this matters anymore. I am done with all of this."

"But, this doesn't seem like a reason big enough to give away your career, your education, your future, does it? Why are you really doing this?"

"I can't sustain this level of isolation for long. There are things I can't stop thinking about from my past either. Things which I have never told you. I feel like I am locked in and have nowhere to go."

"Do you think you can share with me now? Maybe I can help in some way."

"No. I just need to go home and be with my family."

"I understand. Are you close to your family?" I asked hesitantly.

He remained silent for a moment. Then he spoke.

"It's not that my loneliness will go away once I am back, but at least it will become bearable. I am close to my mother. I think she is the only person who really understands me. She needs me and I need her. Sorry, it is something you won't understand. My flight is tomorrow."

He left the next day. He was right. I didn't understand what he was going through back then. I was naive. When we reconnected after a year, he told me how difficult the first few months were once he got back. Then he set aside everything and took time to work on himself. He changed careers and dove deeper into art. Today, he is a self-employed illustrator. He has found his voice and it speaks beautifully.

He was not alone. A lot of us go through such dark periods in our life. This is so because our emotional isolation is much more complex than occasional loneliness. We feel lonely when we are temporarily removed from friends and family, but emotional isolation can happen even though we are in their midst. To be emotionally isolated is to be locked in that space of *not being understood*, sometimes for decades. It is to feel that no one hears or sees us for who we are. We occasionally do have intimate conversations with people, but they are few and far between. We realize that our friendships too, are mostly superficial. We share a few good moments with our friends, but never to our heart's content. We hit a roadblock after which we can't seem to sustain any interaction. There is a boundary we *unknowingly* hold. It feels like a wall of fear that says, *"If you let go of all your filters, they will judge you."*

Why can't we let go of all self-control and freely engage? Because we fear being hurt again. This hurt is rooted in our past trauma.[2] Let's see how traumatic experiences are connected to the emotional isolation we often feel in our lives.

Trauma is far more common than we presume. Sometimes events such as a breakup, a divorce or a death of a family member can cause trauma. If we have had such experiences in our life, then our emotional isolation can be profound. Severe trauma (such as emotional, physical, or sexual abuse) can adversely affect the healthy functioning of our nervous system. It alters the way we perceive our own emotions. Two of these effects seem to have a large impact on our emotional isolation. The first effect is hyper-sensitivity; the second is the opposite—numbness.

Those of us who are hyper-sensitive prefer social isolation. Our pain is easily stirred by the mention of an incident, recurrence of a thought or experiencing of certain physical sensations. Therefore, we want to be left alone, for being alone makes us feel safe. We seek this solitude more, and this physical withdrawal soon turns into an emotional isolation. Those among us who experience numbness because of trauma, also face a similar fate. We struggle to feel an intense emotion the way we expect it to feel. Desire, fear, pain, love, all seem powerless to move us. We feel apathetic and aloof towards people in our lives. We may feel disconnected or dissociated from our own reality. This too ensures that we are unable to

---

[2] We will address trauma in this book indirectly. It's a deep subject in itself and as such, falls outside the scope of this book.

connect with others, we can't respond to their emotional needs the way we expect to. So, this effect plunges us into depths of emotional isolation too.

Whether related to trauma or not, our emotional isolation ensures that all new experiences bring up worry, nervousness, fear and unease. Simple acts such as answering a call, having a casual conversation, meeting someone new or interacting with a superior at work, brings up resistance and anxiety. We become preoccupied with how others are perceiving us, rather than how we are. We constantly feel exposed and vulnerable. This lack of safety affects our self-esteem, our confidence and all our relation-ships. All our actions become infused with hesitation and nervousness. This is the birth of anxiety.

Anxiety arises when we know we are about to face a problem and we have no help. The feeling of being alone with a problem triggers it. When our mind perceives that it has no one it can rely upon, it becomes nervous, afraid, and worried even in moments that don't warrant those feelings. Not only does remaining in a relationship, or an extended project (like a graduate degree program for my friend), or a job become difficult, but it also becomes hard to look for a new one, if we happen to lose what we currently have.

Moments of nervousness, fear and worry are common in everyone's life, but if we are anxious and isolated, these states become persistent and prolonged. Any attempt to escape only makes them worse. One can't force oneself out of anxiety. It's like a snake that tightens its grip over us, the more we try to escape its grasp. There is no deceiving or fighting it. An anxious mind is therefore at a loss. It doesn't know where or how to find peace and calm. So it tries harder. The more it tries not to be anxious, the more anxious it gets. *It struggles to hold on while refusing to let go.* Vacillating between these extremes puts the mind under chronic mental (and sometimes physical) stress.

For some of us, this back and forth continues for so long that it becomes the new normal; we get accustomed to it. Being stressed or anxious becomes a part of our life. Some of us even feel proud of the levels of stress we can handle and brag about how many hours we can toil for. Once this happens, our mind can no longer be at peace with peace. It gravitates towards exerting and struggling. It perceives stress to be exciting, and pain of struggling to be pleasure. *It would rather be stressed than be carefree, for stress is at least familiar.* It knows how to hold it in the body and begins to crave that feeling. Such a mind enters any new life situation with an expectation of stress.

> If things look easy, it complicates them until it is satisfied with the level of hardship it is comfortable with.

For instance, if our work is stress free, we seek out a more stressful job, even if it makes us unhappier. If our relationship is peaceful, we look for reasons to generate conflict. We start unnecessary arguments, obsess over small things, or push away our partner without reason. We love drama, because that creates emotional isolation and stress. If our body is in great health, we eat unhealthy things to go back to feeling unhealthy. If a goal is about to succeed, we derail it and invite failure.

If there are a hundred reasons to succeed, we find that one reason to fail. We snatch defeat from the jaws of victory.

Our isolated, anxious and a stressed mind is trapped from both ends. On one hand, we are facing ordinary life challenges, which are difficult as it is, and on the other, it is unable to fully express its pain to those in its support structure. So some of us develop coping mechanisms such as stress-eating, substance abuse, or obsessive-compulsive behaviors to alleviate some of this inward pressure. These mechanisms, however, don't address the root cause, but only treat the symptoms. Therefore our stress builds up and eventually erupts in the form of outbursts aimed at the people we love.

What happens if our mind is emotionally isolated, anxious and stressed for a long time? What happens if we have no legitimate outlets, such as art, exercise or other activities to release this pressure? Then we have no alternative but rely on temporary measures of alleviating it. We slowly gravitate towards quicker and increasingly efficient means of release. We open the door to uncontrolled pleasure-seeking or addictions.

7
Addictive Behaviors

When we are addicted, our mind and body feel like two pendulums striking each other as they try to stabilize, but in turn only keep knocking each other out of balance.

As we saw in the previous chapter, we gravitate towards pleasure when we feel overwhelmed with stress. However, this doesn't seem to be true for all of us. Not all of us who are stressed are addicted, and not all of us who are addicted had any stress to begin with. This is so because addictions have a variety of causes such as a predisposition due to family history or early exposure to substances, to name a few. Most of these causes lie beyond the scope of this book. For the inquiry we are undertaking, we are concerned mainly with addictive behaviors that arise in the process of escaping one's stress.

We all undergo varying degrees of stress in our lifetime. Some of it comes from anxiety, but a lot of it is also a result of living in a complex human society, with ever-decreasing resources available for each one of us. As a result, each one of us has to work harder, take on more risk, put in more effort and suffer more pain. All these factors contribute to the stress we feel collectively as a society. There is often no other way to release this stress but to seek sensory pleasures to numb ourselves. Although we don't seem to go this route until a certain condition is fulfilled. That condition is an imbalance in our inner equilibrium or well-being.

Each one of us has a subjective understanding of this equilibrium. We can think of it as a *baseline of well-being*. It isn't necessarily the ideal state we want to be in, but a minimum state of well-being we desire. We are in this state when our life is relatively free of problems and the levels of various neurotransmitters and hormones in our body are balanced. When our stress level increases, our well-being drops below this baseline, and negative feelings begin to appear: frustration, anger, lethargy, sadness, boredom, lack of being valued and emotional isolation. Naturally, we want to find our way back up to our baseline equilibrium. The fastest way to get there is often by creating a rush of neurotransmitters and hormones which control this feeling of well-being.

This is why we eat chocolates, start shopping or begin to drink or smoke when we are alone and stressed. We are simply trying to increase our well-being and to get us back over the baseline.

The activities themselves matter little in the beginning; what matters is how they make us feel.

Sensory pleasures don't bother us with questions or conditions, they simply fulfill a need. They answer our call for pleasure, without fail. They set us free from our chains for a few minutes every day, without asking much in return.

If drugs, sex or sugary foods required a lot of energy investment from us, we wouldn't be able to use them. For instance, how much energy does it require to open a tub of ice cream as compared to cooking a delicious meal? That's why it's rare for us to seek pleasure through energy-intense activities, like reading, painting, exercising or creating music. These *active* pleasures require time and commitment. Why would anyone ever try those when *passive* pleasures such as binge-watching television, mindlessly scrolling social-media or pornography are so readily available?

As our stress keeps rising, our inner well-being keeps dropping. The more it drops, the more pleasure is required to raise it back up to the baseline. The steeper the drop, the more urgent the need. This is why potent substances, such as alcohol and drugs, can go from being occasional escapes to regular habits in no time. They become our vices. If left unchecked, they become addictions.[3] Since all of us have a different baseline, we respond to stress in different ways, and not all of us get addicted. How to know if we are addicted. An addiction is marked by repeated cycles of stress and release, lows and highs, frustration and gratification.

Imagine for a moment that we are sculptors who want to carve a figure out of stone. All we have is a chisel and a hammer. As we strike the chisel, it shapes the sculpture. The chisel also becomes dull over time. So with every successive blow, we have to apply more force to the hammer to get the same effect. The more force we use, the more unpredictable the result, and greater is the chance that we damage the sculpture, or hurt ourselves. This is how an addiction works. It becomes increasingly entrenched over time as our sensitivity to pleasure decreases. In order to understand this process better, let's look into the reward cycle that powers an addiction.

The reward cycle.

The reward cycle begins when we feel stressed and fall below our equilibrium of well-being. We then crave pleasure. Our goal is to feel good again and come back to the baseline. However, when we get a pleasurable high we often overshoot that baseline. We feel positively gratified. One day we have one drink, then two, then five never knowing when we will get there. A lot more dopamine or serotonin is released than required in our body, giving us an excessive high each time. This is naturally followed by a steeper crash as our body returns back towards its natural baseline

---

[3] Addiction recovery is a science in itself, and it has a variety of medical treatments available. I am not a medical professional, and any analysis on the subject of addiction presented in this book is unscientific.

Finding Awareness

or equilibrium. As it descends, it falls faster and often ends up *below* the point where it started. This is the dullness we feel after we satisfy an urge. Then the process restarts as this isn't our equilibrium. We feel bored and lethargic and begin to have intense cravings for the same pleasures again. The reward cycle repeats.

This is how we all understand the process to be. But if we look one level deeper, we see the strange interplay between our mind and body that sustains this reward cycle. Let's look at the *same process again,* while underlining the role our thinking plays in this.

When we are feeling dull, we often think unhealthy thoughts that betray our own values and principles. Whether they are about abusing a substance or repeating a behavior is irrelevant. These thoughts often cause immense guilt later. We don't particularly want them, they are just here to serve purpose – to create pleasure. As they fill-up our mind they unbalance it. We see images and visions flash before our eyes as the desire intensifies. This imagination triggers the release of chemicals in the body we saw earlier. As our body moves upwards in well-being, it overshoots. Now since those images have served their purpose, they evaporate and the mind becomes clear. But our body is just beginning its phase of descent. The effect of pleasurable sensations wears off and the body falls below equilibrium. Now, even though we have a balanced and a clear mind, we have an unbalanced and a craving body. Such a body desires pleasure to feel good again and triggers unhealthy thoughts in the mind—destabilizing it—then the whole pattern repeats.

> Once we enter the reward cycle, our mind and body act like two pendulums striking each other as they try to stabilize, but in turn only keep knocking each other out of balance. The mind-body system, as a whole, remains unbalanced. An addictive pattern can therefore become a self-sustaining downward spiral.

There is a brief period between these cycles when both our body and mind somehow return to balance and we find our inner equilibrium. This is the time when our addiction momentarily leaves us alone and we can get things done. The moment our stress levels rise again we get pulled back into our addiction. This is also why a lot of us relapse into our addictive behaviors when traumatic or painful incidents happen. They create a tremendous amount of stress that only our addiction can release.

The remedy

So, what is the way out of this problem of addiction? One (superficial) solution is to undergo detoxification, or starving one's desires, which is to abandon all pleasurable activities and allow the mind and body to return to balance. It's like taking the fuel away from the fire. However, this requires a lot of will power, which is a scarce resource for anyone who is addicted. So pursuing this avenue may only lead to short-term results. A deeper way to assuage this problem is by reducing the amount of stress we are experiencing on a daily basis. To make significant changes to our lifestyle, such as moving away from the city, or leaving a stressful job or a relationship, or living with a family member for a while. It may help us re-engage with society and foster deeper emotional connections with people. These connections fulfill that core desire to connect with other human beings, and in turn reduce our emotional isolation. When we feel connected to others our inner equilibrium becomes stronger and more resilient to stress and, by extension, to addictions.

These are powerful methods to address this problem, yet, they are also incomplete. If the root of addiction, which is emotional isolation, isn't dismantled, the whole machinery of addiction remains intact. That can't be done until we learn how to look at and understand ourselves - a subject of future chapters. So, what happens to a mind caught up in the vicious cycle of addictions? To understand this, we have to dive deeper into the nature of pleasure itself.

NOTE:

In this chapter we looked at the mechanism by which addictions take hold of the mind. However, our understanding of addictions is far from complete. We will explore them more as we go deeper, in Chapter 12: Structure of Suffering, in Chapter 27: The Backwards Law, and ultimately in Chapter 29: Surrender. For now, it may be sufficient to understand that we leave the door open to addictions when we become emotionally isolated from other human beings. While we are on this subject of pleasure-seeking as a means to escape, it also becomes important to note that not all pleasure is the same. Some pleasures may in fact be necessary for our long-term happiness. In the next chapter, let's understand these distinctions better and see what they reveal about the nature of pleasure.

8
The Blind Retriever

Chasing pleasures is like searching for treasures in a cave. You may find some trinkets if you dig around, but who knows what else is lurking there. This cave is our past, and what lies in the shadows, is our fear.

What do we mean by the word pleasure? It is a sensory response to any kind of external or internal stimuli, that can make an organism feel good, comfortable, or at ease with its surroundings. Once we experience a certain pleasure, we remember it. Then in the future, we seek it again if we want to revisit it. This was the idea behind our previous chapter on addictions. They are pleasures we want to keep experiencing over and over again. As such, in the context of this chapter, we will define the word pleasure as *a past experience*, that we want to relive.

This isn't however a universal definition. How we define pleasure depends on who we ask. There may be a reason for it. Pleasure seems to exist on a scale, ranging from comfort on one end – a neutral feeling one has while drinking a glass of clean water – to ecstasy – a blissful delirium produced by a hallucinogen. Most ordinary pleasurable experiences lie

Finding Awareness

somewhere along that spectrum, and so do the definitions of what pleasure constitutes for most of us.

Now, we all need a basic sense of physical and psychological pleasure in our lives in order to get by. We call this basic pleasure security. We need the basics of food, clothing, shelter and a semblance of psychological safety in our day-to-day life, etc. This basic sense of security is the *zero* on our pleasure scale. If we want more pleasure, such as, owning a big house or driving a fast car, we have to move to the right on the pleasure scale based on the particular experience. This concept of the pleasure scale will be useful further in the chapter when we look at the concept of a blind retriever.

In the previous chapter, we saw how sometimes we seek pleasures as a means of escaping our life's problems. However, that's not the only time we pursue pleasures. Many of us pursue them for their own sake. For instance, the pleasure of playing the violin, practicing yoga, painting, reading a book, going for a run, playing chess, cooking or writing are usually undertaken because one enjoys them. Yet, they are also still pleasures. This raises the question *"Are all pleasures fundamentally the same, or is there a crucial difference between the kinds of pleasures we seek?"*

For instance, consider the reward of preparing a gourmet dish, versus the pleasure of eating a big pie (because we were feeling stressed). The first one is an active or creative pleasure, while the second one is a passive or escape pleasure. Both actions make us feel good, but only one of them has the component of enjoyment, practice or creativity to it. One of them is a means to explore, the other, a means to escape.

When we undertake an activity out of love just for the sake of it, we are more involved in the process of exploring and enjoying, rather than gaining any particular pleasure out of it. The focus is on the *process*, not the *outcome*. The pleasure we ultimately experience is a side effect of our main concern, which is engaging in the activity itself. The *means is primary*, while the *end is secondary*. When we are undertaking an activity to escape boredom, lethargy or stress, we are more concerned with the pleasure it provides rather than the nuances of the activity itself. Here, the end goal is primary, while practicing or enjoying the activity is secondary. We could watch *any* movie, eat *any* cake, or purchase *anything*, as long as it helps us forget our worries. *The end justifies the means.*

Why are we examining this? Why does it matter that we understand which pleasures serve what purpose? Aren't active/creative pleasures and passive/escape pleasures the same at the end of the day? Don't they both lead to the same final state? Unfortunately, they don't. There is one more major difference between the two.

Passive/escape pleasures come with adverse consequences, while active/creative pleasures don't.

We saw one such consequence in the previous chapter in regard to our vulnerability to addictions. However, there is another subtle problem they give rise to. Passive or escape pleasures advance us on the negative side of the pleasure scale. As we saw before, the pleasure scale begins at zero, which is a neutral state of basic security or comfort, and extends towards the right, with increasing levels of pleasure. This scale also extends on the other side, to the left of zero. That other side is pain.

Just as we progress on the right side of the scale with desire, we progress on the left side of it with fear.

Our progress on the right is always conscious and deliberate, but our progress on the left side is unconscious and inadvertent. In other words, *seeking pleasure as an escape makes us more susceptible to fear.* Let's find out why.

Why does actively enjoying one's hobby such as painting, not create fear, but passively smoking or drinking does? To understand this, we have to understand the principle of the *'mind as a blind retriever.'* This strange

Finding Awareness

principle at work, makes us tap into our fear, just as we are expecting pleasure. The key to grasping this principle lies in understanding how our mind fetches memories. First, let me tell you a story.

Many years ago I had a friend who had four Labrador retrievers. Among his dogs, only Woody loved to play fetch. He was a chocolate lab with a lustrous coat and a calm demeanor like an old zen master. Even though he was twelve years old and had lost his eyesight due to old age, you could always rely on Woody to get the ball back. What I found curious was how, from a backyard littered with at least 20 tennis balls, Woody could fetch the exact ball which I had just thrown and drop it in front of me.

This was quite puzzling to me as I watched him repeat the act time and time again. When I asked my friend how Woody, being blind, could retrieve so well, my friend told me that's because he didn't need to see. All he needed was his sense of smell. After all, Woody had a powerful nose. He would use a combination of sounds and smells to locate the correct ball. Once I would throw the ball, Woody would start running in the general direction and begin sniffing. After a few minutes, he would know which ball had a fresh human scent on it and bring it back. He didn't care about the color of the ball or whether it was new or old, clean or dirty. All that mattered to him was its scent. If the scent was right, the ball was too.

The more I thought about Woody, the more I felt that his behavior appeared to be quite similar to the way my mind seemed to work. Let's see if Woody's behavior can offer any clues to how we retrieve our memories. If we closely watch how we recall memories, we see that our mind simply fetches them, without paying any particular attention to what those memories contain. Memories are like boxes and our mind is fetching them from the storeroom or basement[4], based on the label on the box, without

---

4   This visual metaphor of the mind being divided into a basement, which stands for the subconscious mind and the living area, which is our conscious mind, is explored in a lot of detail in the chapter on suffering. We are briefly touching upon it here to aid us in our exploration.

actually opening it. What's inside the box is emotions associated with that memory. The label on the box is a trigger for recalling the situation, or identifying the box. It could be a photograph we come across in our closet, or a song we hear in a restaurant, or a human's scent on a tennis ball. Each trigger brings back a certain memory, perhaps of our grandmother, perhaps of someone we knew in school, or perhaps of a lost love.

Our mind simply fetches the box it is meant to, without questioning what's inside it. Just as Woody didn't care about whether the ball was clean or dirty, our mind doesn't care about whether the memory was positive or negative. It simply fetches it, like a blind retriever. When the box is opened, that is, when our body feels the emotions contained in that memory, we register whether the memory was painful or pleasing. If we recall a lullaby our grandmother used to sing, we feel her love and warmth. We register that the memory we just retrieved was positive. However, if we remember an argument we had with her, then we feel sad since the memory was painful. *In neither case did we know in advance what we were fetching. We were blind to the emotions contained within the memory.*

This is why we never say, *"I am about to have a negative thought"* but *"I had a negative thought."* We only know once it has already happened. Our mind doesn't know good from bad memories, pleasing from painful memories, until it's too late. Like a blind retriever, it simply fetches what it is asked to. When I would pick up the ball, Woody had fetched, I would know if it was dirty or clean, only *after* he had fetched it. His job was simply to retrieve.

How does this explain the adverse consequences of passive/escape pleasures?

> When we teach our minds to retrieve pleasurable memories – as is the case specifically with passive/escape-pleasures – we are also teaching it to spend a lot of time in our past.

Finding Awareness

We tend to forget that both pain and pleasure reside there. We go there looking for pleasure (which is a known pleasing experience), but we also come in contact with pain. If we refuse to stay in the present and spend a lot of time in the past, chasing mindless pleasures, we make ourselves vulnerable to pain too. Remember, the mind is blind to the contents of our memories. So it can pick up a painful memory, as easily as it can a pleasant one. The more time we spend in the past, the more opportunities we give for our pain to arise, unannounced. This is why the more pleasure we chase, the more we find casually thinking about our painful past too. The floodgates to the past are opened.

Looking for pleasure in our past experiences is therefore a dangerous choice. It is like looking for treasures in a cave. You may find some trinkets if you dig around, but who knows what else is lurking there?

Think of someone who is learning to ride a bicycle with a support wheel only on the right side. They lean on the right (desire/pleasure) and keep riding, because there is a wheel here that holds them. They believe they are safe. When the wind starts blowing in the opposite direction, they now fall to the left (fear/pain). They never trained for balance, so they are bound to fall on the left.

Engaging in passive/escape pleasures is like conditioning ourselves to lean (towards the past or the future), without training to find balance (in the now).

This is why active pleasures, which includes our pursuit of our hobbies, such as reading, writing, painting, cooking or exercising play an important role. ***They provide us pleasure without making us vulnerable to fear***. They are not based on accessing the past. They are about being in the present. Even though they may require using some memory associated with skill (eg., remembering how to play an instrument), the goal is to use that memory to create joy in the present.

So if we chase pleasures, we arrive at yet another intractable problem; that of fear. We saw that fears are recollected more easily if we train our mind to recall pleasure since they both rooted in the past. However, we did *not* say that pleasure-seeking is the reason why our fears exist. Our fears were born elsewhere. The source of our fears is our painful past. Now that we are here, let's understand our fears next, and see where this exploration leads.

> NOTE:
>
> The blind retriever principle shows us that pleasure and pain are two sides of the same coin, just as desire and fear. They lie on the opposite side of the pleasure scale. If we seek one, we end up with the other. In some sense there is a balance here. We saw in the previous chapters how stress makes us want to balance it with pleasure. Now, we see how going overboard with pleasure, sends us back in the direction of fear. There is a beautiful symmetry in this phenomena. The good and the bad, the positive and negative seem to not only be in conflict, but also in harmony.

9
Fear

Fear is a hallucination that makes it seem as if a distant future or a past is present and real.

We have various kinds of fears in our life: Fear of not finding true love; of being hurt again; of loneliness; of failure; of losing one's job; of failing in our relationships; of physical pain; of darkness; of not arriving on time; of the unknown; phobias of various kinds; and lastly, of fear itself. Fear is an immense roadblock to living the life we want. It follows us like a shadow. Most of us struggle to navigate our fears. There is rarely ever a feeling of being completely free of them. We rarely wake up in the morning and draw back the curtains to see only clear blue skies. There is at least one dark cloud somewhere in the distance.

The first solutions we try to overcome our fears are feigning courage, holding on to faith, or thinking positive thoughts. This is understandable. These methods have their benefits in the short term, but they are hardly enough to get us through our entire lives. For instance, courage is always in conflict with fear. A part of us is afraid while the other part is pretending not to be. This inward rejection of our reality makes our life a perpetual battle. The more fears we have, the more we have to put on.

Finding Awareness

If the fear is powerful, it can be exhausting to keep telling oneself to be courageous.

Faith tends to work better than courage. It can help us relax in the moment. It doesn't eradicate fear, but helps us cover it up and protect it. It requires us to cling to an idea in the hope that things will work out. When faith enters the scene, we don't have to change ourselves anymore. Everything is taken care of. It absolves us of our responsibilities. Fear in the meanwhile keeps growing, and so does faith in order to keep it under wraps. Soon, everything in our life becomes a matter of faith. If we lose a job or need help in our relationship, our faith may prevent us from seeking help, for faith admits no fault whatsoever. Doubt weakens faith. So, the first casualty when faith arrives is our ability to doubt anything. Then faith continues to cover up a grim reality with comforting words and ideas.

These coping methods don't seem to work because they arise from the same source, which is *our desire to be free of fear*. A desire to be free of fear, is fear too, right? It's the fear of fear itself. So we already have made our first mistake. We have asked one fear to resolve other fears. We have asked a thief to guard our house. Nothing good can come of that. Perhaps that explains why we find ourselves where we are. We have practiced all these methods for decades, and still live deeply in the clutches of fear.

So let's try a different approach this time; one which isn't trying to get rid of fear but only trying to observe and understand it.

Types of Fears

When we observe our fears, we realize that they are not all the same. There are three main types: survival fears (fear of imminent physical danger), psychological fears (fear of experiencing the pain from our past and the future), and neurotic fears (phobias).

Survival fears are those that make us afraid of darkness, wild animals, heights, drowning, physical confrontations, or bodily harm. During any of these situations our immediate survival is at stake. For instance, we find ourselves unable to swim in deep water, we confront a bear on a hike, or we get into a fight with someone. These are all situations where our lives are in danger. Our body goes into a state of fight or flight while all our senses have a single purpose: to protect our life.

Then there are psychological fears that prevent us from living the life we want. Fear of embarrassment, social rejection, inability to pursue our dreams, heartbreak, unemployment, failure at an important project, abandonment by our partner, entrapment with a wrong partner, being unmarried, and the death of a loved one all fall in this club.

Then we have the third type, which are our phobias. Some of us dread spiders, public speaking, large crowds, air travel, needles, the sight of blood, domestic animals, etc. to such an extent that they prevent us from leading a fulfilling life. They may arise from a traumatic event in childhood or even a genetic predisposition. Once a phobia[5] occurs, it can make ordinary life situations difficult.

So, those are the three types. Now, let's look at survival and psychological fears a little closer and see what they reveal about us.

Survival fears are a function of nature. They helped our ancestors avoid dangerous predators, steep cliffs, brightly colored snakes, toxic plants, and so on. The longer they survived, the more they passed on these fears, both genetically and behaviorally, to their descendants. These fears are like life-saving biological rules we follow without questioning. All species of animals have them. Therefore, these fears don't need any overcoming at all, as they are here to help us. They are normal, healthy, and essential.

This leaves us with psychological fears. When this type of a fear is active, we find ourselves picturing a negative outcome. Images of us failing

---

[5] Phobias are outside the scope of this book, however they need mentioning. Phobias defy introspection and analysis, and only respond to progressive and slow exposure to them. Each phobia is unique and requires a different treatment, and as such any method we discover here can't apply to them all. They need targeted treatment from a medical professional or even individual experimentation to see what works.

at our goals, losing our job, or divorcing our partner flash before our eyes. As we conjure these images, we rarely stop and ask where they are coming from. If we can visualize someone leaving us, how do we know what that might look like? If we are afraid of being lonely, how do we know what loneliness feels like?

Upon asking such a question, we realize that these images come from our own (or from watching someone else's) past. We are using our memories as building blocks to manufacture a negative future. We are unknowingly projecting our past onto our future. For example, when we were children, we had no concept of failure. We weren't afraid to take on new hobbies, meet new people, or ask questions. If we were angry, we screamed. If we were sad, we cried. We lived in the moment. It was only when we had hurtful experiences growing up did we start developing our fears. We began spending more and more time in our past as it grew. If our past was hurtful, we felt afraid. This is why each one of us has a different set of fears, for we all have a unique personal history.

A psychological fear can only be recreated from our past memories. If there was a way to erase those negative memories, our fears would instantly disappear too. These fears have no independent existence; they rely on our past memories. In other words, fear is a *powerful hallucination that makes it seem as if a painful event from our past is about to repeat itself.*

If you have a certain fear you'd like to examine, hold it in your mind and just to look at it. What you are witnessing is your past life. Notice how fear *requires* that you leave the present moment and become occupied with those frightening images from your past. Witness how the mind is creating this phantasm from nothing in this present moment. You have seen suffering, and you are imagining that you will suffer again. Yet, in this moment, none of it is real.

Fear creates an anticipation of suffering. *This anticipation of pain is far worse than actual pain.* It offers to prepare us for what's coming. This preparation has to be understood, for it contains a struggle which has its own travail. Medical professionals are well aware of it. This is why they distract the patients before putting them under anesthesia, before administering an injection, or resetting a bone. They want to calm the patient's nerves by *not preparing* them for what's about to happen.

> Preparing not to suffer brings its own form of suffering, for it's impossible to be fully prepared.

If we observe the painful situations we have undergone, it often seems that perhaps we handled ourselves well while in the middle of them. Our mind had adjusted to the pain and was helping us get through those tough days. What makes our past experience seem more harrowing now, is our analysis in hindsight. For instance, a broken relationship is always painful, but it seems much more painful when we reminisce about it. Perhaps if we don't know of the suffering that's coming our way, we may be able to suffer in dignity, for expecting pain does nothing to reduce it.

Fear in relationships

How does fear affect our relationships? Fear is such an integral part of living that it soon becomes a sort of basic expectation from other people. We expect to see fear in others, for its existence indicates normalcy. What seems abnormal to us is someone living without fear. For instance, some of us are wary of those who don't fear a god or a higher power. When someone is a *'god-fearing man (or woman),'* it puts our heart at ease. This is because knowing someone's fears helps us understand them in ways few other things can. When you understand someone's fears, you can also control their behavior to suit your needs. Human beings have done this to other humans for centuries.

Parent-child relationships

Our parents have conditioned us this way too. For instance, *"Get married soon or you'll always be lonely,"* or *"Don't drop out of college, otherwise*

I won't support you," or *"Do your homework or you'll fail the subject."* These are common warnings we all have heard. These statements always took the form of *"do this or face that consequence."* They scared us into doing things that we wouldn't have. This is how we become conditioned by our fears. They are such a normal part of our life that we take them for granted. They become part of our identities.

Some of these fears get passed down out of love, others out of ignorance. We touched upon this in the first chapter too. Overprotective parents pass on their fears to their children. These fears often hide underneath religious or political beliefs, principles, values or anything else they can hide under. *These fears make the child's life difficult, but the parent's life easier.* They give the parents a (false) sense of security, which says, *"I did my best to protect my children."*

Negligent parents pass on their fears to their children too. Fear of being cheated in relationships, of abandonment, of commitment, of not being valued, of being insulted or bullied, of being unable to chase your dreams, are all fears that can be inherited. Children pick these fears up not by listening to what their parents say, for they often don't say much, but by watching their actions. This is fear-conditioning. We can consider ourselves fear-conditioned if we fear things because we were taught to fear them, regardless of what our personal experience says.

When fear-conditioned children enter society as adults, they come in contact with other like-minded individuals. When others are as afraid of the same things as they are, it creates a camaraderie. Since connecting with other human beings is a core need, why it happens is of little relevance to us. Fear works just as well as anything else. Notice how when someone displays the same fears as us – about the state of the world, or about not being heard or seen – we instantly feel a connection with them. We feel as if they 'get it.' They have the same opinions as us, so we huddle together. We embrace each other for the emotional warmth it provides. When fear is the primary means of connection between such like-minded people, they can form (ideological, religious or political) groups bound by the threads of their shared fears. *They develop a fear bond that gives them a (false) sense of security.*

A fear bond is created every time we connect with someone based on our shared set of fears. It makes us feel secure, without having to deal with our fears. A similar thing happens in our intimate relationships too.

Intimate relationships

If we have fears of being abandoned, we easily get attracted to someone who shares the same fears. Our connection is magical, instant, and deep. This person feels unique and special, for who else would understand our fears and insecurities so deeply, unless they were *'the one'*? We begin to depend on them and they on us. We feel bound to each other. We suffer with them, yet no other alternative makes any sense. This is why our codependent relationships make us feel both secure and insecure at the same time.

The security is false, coming out of a fear-bond, and the insecurity, real.

So now we ask the next question: What happens when this (false) security provided by the fear-bond is threatened? For instance, what happens when one partner challenges the other to get rid of their insecurities and fears? This sparks a conflict between the two. For when we are secure (falsely or not) in a certain place, it becomes impossible to move out of it without a conflict. We feel threatened or attacked by our partner and wonder if the relationship has run its course. The relationship enters a difficult phase as the verbal and psychological violence towards each other increases. We argue over small things, protect our opinions, lash out angrily, or shut out our partner – all various forms of violence. So the moment our (false) security is threatened, we become more violent in our relationships. If we are violent, our partner has no choice but to protect themselves so they respond in kind. Fear transforms into violence in relationships.

The same violence is manifested on a global scale, when two fear-based identities collide in the form of religions, political ideologies, or nations. Fear creates war. We begin to realize that once fear takes hold of our mind, violence is not far behind. This threatens the security of everyone involved in that relationship.

The root of fear

What is at the root of fear? Why did we bond with another person, intimately or not, in the first place? It was because we were searching for security, weren't we? We were seeking refuge. We felt afraid in the moment, so we said, *"I must not be afraid tomorrow. I must secure my future."* Security is a basic need without which we cannot live. So does this mean that we are condemned to be stuck with our fears and the false security our fear-bonds provide?

No, we aren't. This becomes clear when we understand that feeling protected, safe and secure is a desire that can only be fulfilled in the present, not in the future. Our mind gets tricked into thinking that it must try and secure its future, which is an impossible task and, therefore, it gets caught in an endless struggle. The only way to secure the future is to make it the *past*. Otherwise the future will always be unpredictable and, therefore, a cause for fear. We saw this in the chapter on unfairness too. In our obsession with the future, we end up ignoring the present and can't find *real* security. *This continuous lack of security in the present moment manifests itself as a never-ending fear.* We keep chasing the mirage of future security, when there is no such thing. What we need is security in the present moment, which is possible. *Security can only exist now. The idea of seeing oneself secure in the future is an illusion.*[6] We will never be secure tomorrow, we can only be secure today and now.

---

6   This raises more questions about whether planning for our future has any value. We will look at this question in Chapter 26: Presence and Planning when we look at positive thinking and planning as a means to change.

NOTE:

Just because a codependent relationship provides (false) security, doesn't mean we need to end it. There are ways which can help us transform our codependent relationship into a secure one. That way points to finding security in ourselves, so we don't have to rely on our partner for it. One way to look at it is to see ourselves as two broken cups trying to use the fragments of each other to mend themselves. It can't be done, for both the cups broke in different ways and are made of a different material. They can't complete each other no matter how hard they try. They can only complete themselves. How does one complete oneself? This whole book is an attempt to answer that question. Let's carry on with our self-inquiry, for asking the right questions, is far more important than finding the right answers.

10
The Violence Within

Every expectation we have from our partner is perceived by them as an unspoken threat.

My friend and I sat in the backyard of my house as the sun was setting and the crickets began to chirp. He was visiting after many months. As always, our discussions veered into philosophy and matters related to the human condition. We spoke about many subjects that evening and had arrived at this moment after a good two hours of intense discussions. As I threw some wood in the fire pit, he said, *"Perhaps violence is something so innate to human beings that we will never know its true cause. We are a violent species, what else is there to know? Human history is a history of wars."*

I nodded in agreement. *"I don't know if we will ever be able to stop it,"* I added. *"Perhaps we will always be a violent species. We don't know the root of violence, so when it happens, we are helpless. We just carry it out."*

It seemed as if there was nothing more left to discuss. Our conversation was drawing to a close, as was the evening light. The night was almost upon us. The insects in the large ash tree under which we happened to be sitting were getting louder by the minute. A crescendo rose and fell as thousands of crickets and cicadas chirped in unison. We settled into the rhythm of their song, and the soft crackling and popping of firewood. It's not often that your best friend comes visiting. I took a deep breath and sunk deeper into my chair, enjoying this lull in our talk.

Then, out of nowhere, a cicada came buzzing down the ash tree and sat on my left arm. Just as it landed, my right hand whisked it off without a moment's delay. Visceral fear and panic gripped me. As it landed next to my foot, it began its loud whirring and whizzing. I had a strong urge to kick it away. I lifted my foot, but then hesitated. I glanced at my friend who was calmly holding his wineglass up in the air, as if to make a toast. He had a cold smile on his face. *"To violence,"* he said as he waited for me. I sat down and left the insect alone. I picked up my glass and replied, *"To non-violence,"* and we both drank to it.

The cicada was still buzzing next to my foot, making crackling noises, testing my resolve and inciting the violence within. I took a deep breath and let that unpleasantness sink in. *"This is the root of violence, fear,"* a thought said. The insect flew away and all was still.

Most of us believe that we are not of a violent disposition and that we wouldn't physically attack or hurt anyone, even in our wildest dreams. Yet, when our mind experiences fear or danger, violence isn't always a conscious choice. Our reaction to an immediate danger is always one of the three: fight, flight or freeze. The flight-or-freeze response doesn't do anything about the threat we are facing. However the fight reaction is unique. It takes matters into its own hands. We resist the threat. This is where our violent responses come from. If we can understand this process, perhaps we can transcend the violence within us.

What happens when someone cuts us off while driving, belittles our opinion, speaks behind our backs, or violates our trust? We respond with immediate hostility and anger. When someone insults us or implies something about us that isn't true, it makes us feel weak. We feel helpless in changing the way they are thinking about us. This inability to change their mind and the unfolding situation makes us feel powerless. This is an unpleasant feeling for most of us. As a result, we make a split-second decision to take that power back.

We do this through anger and aggression.

> Anger instantly makes us feel powerful.
> That's why it is usually perceived as a sign of weakness.

Only in a weak state of mind do we need anger to make things go our way. An angry person rarely admits that they arrived there because they felt afraid or powerless. They feel justified in the way they feel. Anger is our last resort to gain control over a situation that's getting out of hand. This anger however, is a transitory phase. It is preparing our mind for something worse – violence.

Once anger erupts, it quickly turns into verbal or non-verbal violence. Violence is like fire. It burns everything it touches. This is why we have a responsibility to understand and let go of our psychological fears, or else we risk becoming violent individuals. How does fear lead to violence in our relationships?

Violence in relationships

Our primary fear in relationships is that of having unfulfilled expectations. Sometimes we rely on our partners to be our emotional bedrocks. We want them to appreciate us, support us in our spiritual growth, and take more responsibility for their own growth. We expect them to let go of their egoic thinking, and share or support us in our hobbies and passions. If so, we are setting ourselves up to become victims of fear and violence. To understand why, first let's look at how our expectations hurt us more than they help us.

What happens when our partner doesn't do what we expect them to? We become hurt and resentful. We criticize, blame, argue, accuse and challenge them. Some of us shut down all conversation. We are not really working to improve our communication; we are simply using our silence to hurt our partner. Each method we use to get back at them is a form of subtle, yet deliberate, violence we inflict upon them. We become sarcastic, accusatory, or defensive.

So what do our partners do in return? When they feel this attack coming from us, they start building an emotional barrier to protect themselves. It is only natural for them to do so. We threatened them with repercussions. With many cycles of unmet expectations and violent follow-ups, they begin to perceive each expectation as a hidden assault on their way of being. They defend themselves by becoming avoidant and unavailable. Sometimes they blame and criticize us for the tension in the relationship. They call us insecure, sensitive or selfish. In other words, they end up creating a counter threat for us. Once we are intimidated by their behavior we have no option but to repeat their mistake. We erect emotional barriers to protect ourselves too. This back and forth cycle continues for years and each person isolates themselves more and more as time goes on. This is how a relationship starts with openness but ends up in conflict.

Expectation as a threat

Two people who love each other often move apart because they fail to realize that each expectation they had from their partner was being perceived by them as an unspoken threat. Why do we expect things from others? What are these expectations after all? Is expecting your partner to do the dishes, or the laundry, or take care of your baby too much to ask for? Can't we expect these basic things from our partner, especially if they took on these responsibilities along with us as equal participants? Shouldn't they put in their fair share of effort in the relationship?

They absolutely should. However, communicating those needs as expectations paints them as threats. They become subtle acts of violence. If we communicate these expectations as clear needs we have, without the impending anger or resentment, then our partner perceives them neutrally without feeling as if they are being attacked. They feel spoken to and heard at the same time. Why aren't we able to communicate our expectations this way? Why is it so difficult to practice calm communication? Why is anger our first response?

This is because deep down we are under a constant threat too! As we saw in the chapter on insecurity, when we are insecure, we feel as if we are always being attacked. As such our responses are trying to protect ourselves. This makes calm communication impossible. Naturally, we speak in threats. Even if we don't say a word, our body language and facial expression betray our violent thoughts. Our partners, being quite perceptive in these matters, can sense this impending attack. So this all comes back full circle. In essence, *if we can't create our own security, we unknowingly lean on our partner and that sends us both down the wrong path.*

In some sense *we don't have relationship problems at all; we have self-knowledge and security problems.* Over the length of this book, that is the journey we are undertaking. To see if through self-inquiry we can reach the end of our fears and our insecurities and be that guiding light to ourselves, which we look for in others. We haven't gotten there yet. Let's assume for a moment that we do, then how do our relationships look? How do they transform if there was no self-betrayal or insecurity in our lives?

Then we don't set forth any conditions or expectations from our partners, only clear needs when necessary. When they hear us calmly communicating our needs, they begin to feel more relaxed and accepted in our presence. They notice this sudden freedom they have been given and desire more of it. They change their behavior. They take down their defensive barriers, and become willing to lean forward in their efforts. They also begin to share their deepest thoughts and vulnerabilities. They become more open to ideas and suggestions they had so far rejected.

Finding Awareness

As they become more vulnerable, we too begin to perceive the end of violence in our relationship, and start listening to what they have to say. As the walls come down, space is created. This space can be filled with genuine care, affection and love. We can now support each other through our troubles and work towards our dreams. A new cycle of reconnection and togetherness begins. The distance between two people begins to close and the relationship begins to heal. The beauty of this process is that it only takes one person to walk this path and that person is always you.

> NOTE:
> Expectations are also related to an aspect of relationships we are yet to examine: our attachments. We will study attachments in a later chapter when we assess the structure of our ego. There, we shall clarify which expectations are born of attachments, and which aren't. Without understanding attachments and its relationship with fear and insecurity, this process of reconnecting with ourselves (and therefore our partners) remains incomplete. Yet, if we voluntarily keep aside our expectations once in a while and experiment with not having our way, we see positive changes unfold. To let go of violence is difficult, but it can be done. When it happens, we feel a profound shift in our relationships.

11
Hurt Cycles – Guilt and Regret

If we are unable to resolve our hurt, we subconsciously believe that the only way to make others understand us is to hurt them too.

Hurt plays a strange role in our life. With too little of it, we don't quite know how the real world functions. With too much of it, the world appears to be a dangerous place. Hurt is one of the main consequences of violence we inflict on each other. A majority of our pain comes from what other people have done to us or have failed to do for us.

Hurt

What is hurt? Simply put, it's a memory of pain which is hard to release. We were hurt when we were told that we weren't smart, patient, kind or good enough as a child. We remember the times we were told that we cried too much or weren't as smart as our siblings. We felt neglected when our parents seemed more interested in solving their own problems than raising us. We were traumatized when we were bullied at school or when our partner broke our trust. If someone hurts us, our first reaction is to get back at them. Most of us want retribution. But what if we can't have it? What if the person isn't around for us to hurt anymore? What if it's too late to bring up what they did to us when we were children? What if they are in a position of power at work? What happens to our hurt then? It sinks deeply into our subconscious mind and makes a home there.

We want to ensure that we never get caught again, like we did back then. We have no choice. We become quick-tempered and hypersensitive. In this process, sometimes we accidentally end up hurting those who are close to us. We hurt them for no fault of theirs and no fault of ours. This is how a hurt cycle propagates, spreading the pain across many lives, sometimes many generations. Everyone wants to have the last word and it keeps the cycle going.

For instance, those who have *unresolved* hurt in their lives often tend to make the lives of others hard, as they follow in their footsteps. We can see this in the workplace where someone who has advanced after hardships doesn't let others advance easily. They feel jealous about someone else's quick progress and try to slow them down. Difficult co-workers or bosses are often just regular people sharing their hurt with us the only way they know best – by making us go through the same adversities they did. They don't believe that others deserve the same success they got for a less amount of effort.

We see this in a family dynamic as well. Parents who had strict or abusive childhoods sometimes perpetuate that harshness onto their children, using the pretext of making them understand the *value of hard work* or *earning their success.* Their childhoods were painful, and yet they seemed to have made it. So what could possibly go wrong with making their children's lives full of privations too? If they were hit or spanked by their parents, they see nothing wrong with doing the same to their children. After all, they turned out to be non-violent adults, right?

If we are unable to resolve our pain, we subconsciously believe that the only way to make others understand us, is to hurt them too. Sharing our heartache reduces the total burden we all carry, but only if there is compassion in our hearts. Otherwise we are increasing the shared pain of humanity by perpetuating the hurt cycle.

Guilt

In the process of getting back at people for hurting us, sometimes we lose control over ourselves and overreact, we come to repent our actions. This leads us into another aspect of our suffering, regret and guilt.

Guilt is caused by two main reasons: when we realize that we have hurt someone or when we find out that we had a moral or ethical failure. In both scenarios, we became someone else. We fell prey to a fear or a desire. We made a mistake which is unforgivable in our own eyes.

> Guilt feels as if we can't forgive ourselves;
> nor can we atone for what we did.

We are trapped in the middle. Guilt, in essence, is an impossible desire. It is a wish that the past was different. This is why it blocks our mental energy. We keep asking the same question over and over again: *"What could I have done differently?"* We keep going back to the incident, replaying it like a never ending movie. We analyze everything and agonize over each detail. Sometimes we vacillate between justification and condemnation, defiance and regret.

This is why guilt sometimes lingers for years. Its purpose isn't to change *future behavior*, but to change *past behavior*. So wouldn't it make sense for us to let go of all the guilt? Yes it would, and yet we can't. *We have been conditioned by society to believe that repentance is more important than transformation.* Our society has weaponized guilt as a tool against anyone who breaks its norms and to punish them for the rest of their lives. We love to hold those who falter accountable, then wonder why forgiveness and redemption are hard to come by, when *we* need it.

Finding Awareness

Guilt in relationships

When regret, shame or guilt become part of our intimate relationships, our ability to heal gets entangled in our partners' ability to forgive. We may have undergone a genuine transformation, yet there is no easy way to regain that trust we lost. We have felt genuine remorse; we changed our behaviors, mastered our anger and controlled our desires. Yet, if our partner is not able to move on, they impose the burden of guilt upon us. Trust is a brittle, delicate thing – like glass. It's hard to build, and easy to crack. Once it shatters, we often have to start all over again.

If we expect our partner to forgive us, we fall back into the same trap we discussed in the previous chapter. That expectation feels like a threat to them, and they can't forgive us. So what is the solution to guilt? It is to find forgiveness within oneself for what happened, not in our partner. Then the next question becomes how do we forgive ourselves? Unfortunately, we can't *decide* to forgive ourselves. Such a decision can't bring genuine forgiveness, but only a verbal pretense. It is at best, superficial. We can only observe and understand ourselves in such a way that one day we look back and realize that forgiveness has already happened. It happens when we profoundly realize that there was nothing we could have done. We will look at this process in more detail in Chapter 24 when we question our beliefs. In any case, whether our partner forgives us or not, is never in our hands. Their journey has always been their own, and our responsibility is to let them complete it, in their own time.

Note:

As we approach the end of this section, we have taken a journey into the nature of our suffering. We have watched it become a central theme of our lives. We rarely ask, *"Why am I happy?"* but we do ask, *"Why do I suffer?"* Suffering is the only reason why we ever admit that perhaps we don't know everything about ourselves or the world. When we suffer, we become more willing to listen. It comes in many forms: loneliness, insecurity, fear, regret, hurt, pain or pleasure, all of which we have examined in depth. Now, let's try to understand how our mind stores this suffering and see what it reveals about us.

12
The Structure of Suffering

Every painful memory that arises in our mind points to an unresolved experience trying to resolve, or complete itself.

One of my regular readers asked if we could speak in person, saying in advance that he wanted to talk about the nature of suffering and happiness. Our first conversation began with this observation:

"*Suffering seems to be the main theme in your writings,*" he said.

"*Yes it is. It's the central aspect of life. It has a deeper meaning than enjoyment or happiness,*" I replied.

"*But isn't happiness the end goal? Why focus on this subject of suffering so much?*"

"*Happiness is not the end goal for a lot of people. They are looking for something more reliable, like meaning and significance to their life. In any case, happiness or meaning are both fair goals. Just that if this process of suffering isn't understood, they remain out of reach. If we don't understand suffering, we just keep creating more of it in our lives.*"

"*So, are you suggesting that seeking happiness is a waste of time?*"

Finding Awareness

"It depends on what we mean by happiness. Most of the time, our search for happiness is nothing more than seeking pleasure in different forms. That's just escaping from our problems. Seeking wealth, leisures, and comfort is what most think of when we think of happiness. Few of us can think of it without associating it with owning more possessions. It's not real happiness at all, but acquisitiveness. When we lose things for some reason, they become sources of pain.

If your source of happiness can be converted to a source of pain, then it's just an attachment.

Nothing more. So looking for happiness without understanding suffering just creates more pain. This is because happiness is the end of suffering. It's what's left behind. We don't have to seek it separately. Occasionally, we feel this when we stop resisting whatever is happening both inside and outside, like when we look at a beautiful sunset. Otherwise, everything we seek is just a fleeting pleasure, which we label happiness."

"I see what you're saying. So then how do I proceed? I feel stuck," he replied.

"We proceed not by trying to be happy, but by trying to understand our suffering."

"So how do I understand my suffering? Can you elaborate on what it's made of? Everything I read about it makes me want to not look at it. It's a little depressing. You seem to think that suffering is in some way interesting to you."

"Suffering is beautiful to look at. It ends all self-deception and makes us think. It jolts us out of our slumber. Most of us look inward only because we have suffered. You're here, and I am here because of it. If we observe its structure, we see how intricate and elegant it is. Do you want to examine what it's made of? It takes a while to go into but once we see it, it feels obvious and intuitive. It informs every single decision we make in life."

"Yes, let's dive in. What is the structure of suffering?"

The Structure of Suffering

The rest of this chapter is based on our conversation. The three most common ways we suffer are through unresolved hurt, pleasure and fear. Once we understand these three forms of suffering, the rest of them become easy to understand.

The subconscious mind

Our exploration into suffering begins with understanding our subconscious mind. This space is like a basement or a storeroom under a very large house.[7] Here, there are thousands of boxes, where each box represents a memory or an experience. Each box has a color based on the emotion it contains. Let's say we choose blue for *hurt*, red for *fear*, and green for *pleasure*. All boxes are neatly arranged in their respective spaces separated by the different colors.

As we have said earlier in this book, suffering is caused by unresolved emotions. If an emotion is unresolved, the box is open. If it's resolved, the box is closed. We see that some of the blue, green and red boxes are open, while the others are neatly closed. The open boxes are our memories which are still unresolved, and therefore they are creating pain. The closed boxes are our memories which may have been painful at some point, but now they aren't. They are closed. Let's keep going and see how this analogy describes the nature of our suffering. Let's look first at hurt, then at pleasure then at fear.

Hurt

How do we get hurt? Generally this happens when a partner or friend criticizes us for our decisions or views. As we listen, we get angry and snap at them. Once the situation is behind us, we think about what happened over and over again. Why do we mull over it? This *churning the past* happens because when they said those words we weren't prepared for

---

[7] What follows from here on is simply a theory of how suffering works. There is no scientific basis in research for this model of suffering. This is purely to understand at a personal level how our suffering may look. The usage of the word memory, is also a generic usage, and is synonymous with 'past experience.' The usage of the word 'mind', is not to be confused with the brain, which is an organ.

them. We failed to respond to their challenge in real time. That experience was left unfinished because we couldn't express ourselves fully. However, our mind isn't happy with this. It's not satisfied with leaving something incomplete. So what does it do?

It stores this memory in a blue box. This box remains open since the experience is yet unresolved. This is what we commonly refer to as unfinished business or a grudge against someone. It keeps coming up until it's resolved and completed. This *rising up* is the reason why we compulsively think about old events. This is why we brood over painful arguments, hurtful words or memories of loss. We feel this in the form of *uninvited* painful memories appearing in our conscious mind.

In comparison, how does a finished experience look? Had we responded to the situation by being present and centered, then that experience would have been finished or resolved. (We will look at how this happens in the next section, when we look at *centering*.) In that case, the memory would end up in a sealed and closed blue box, with nothing left to be done about it. It would be a *finished* and *resolved* experience. If the experience is resolved, its emotional content becomes inactive. It loses its charge and momentum. Such a resolved memory doesn't create any thoughts, unless we invite it to. If a resolved painful memory is evoked, we remember it without any suffering. This is why we can recall past relationships that ended amicably, or the passing of our grandmother and not feel pain. Our pains heal, when our memories resolve.

Now, let's see if pleasure too can create suffering this way.

Pleasure

An unfinished pleasure is created if one is under stress or avoidance when the experience first happens. For instance, if we consume alcohol under stress or to escape from loneliness, or as a means to fall asleep, then the risk of it becoming an unfinished experience is higher. Then our mind wants to finish that experience later. It keeps thinking about it. An *open green box* is created. This may be one (among many) reasons why some of us can have alcohol and never be addicted to it, while others are. Our core experience relating to alcohol did not happen during a stressful time in our lives.

This is why addictive behaviors tend to have this avoidance at their core. The mind is always running from something. If we are addicted to a substance, we have this persistent feeling that we can't have enough of it. How can we? We weren't really *there* when the experience was happening in the first place. Our mind was divided, so it could never finish that experience. It is now trapped in that state of *trying to finish* that experience, creating multiple incomplete experiences to date. In some ways, we are still trying to finish that first drink. Gradually our brain and body lose their sensitivity and the behavior grows into an addiction.

So how does one resolve such an experience? That pleasure becomes a closed green box, when we experience it deeply, and therefore there is no part of it which is left incomplete. We have to learn how to experience something with intensity or with total presence. We will see this in detail in the chapters on *centering*. This means we have to have that first drink with a high degree of awareness about what we are doing. If we have this heightened awareness while engaging in pleasurable actions, they don't leave that unfinished mark behind. A completed pleasure doesn't generate any more desires or thoughts. There is no allure or seduction left in it. The green box is closed since its contents are now resolved.

Now, we come to our unresolved fears.

Fear

We have studied various aspects of fear and how they relate to our past. However, what we haven't seen is how fear can also be unresolved or resolved. Unresolved fears are those which are *active* fears in our life. If we are currently afraid of being single, losing our job or failing to reach our dreams, our fears are contained in open red boxes. This perfectly fits in

Finding Awareness

with what we had discovered about fear earlier – that it's a hallucination which brings our past back to life. Fear too, stems from our unresolved memories. So our fear, by definition, is unresolved in nature. That is why it keeps generating unwelcome thoughts.

If, over a period of time, we are able to overcome a fear then it transforms into fearlessness. *"I am afraid of uncertainty,"* becomes, *"I am okay with whatever happens."* How this happens, we are yet to see. Though, when it does, our fear is resolved and our past no longer generates fearful thoughts.

> This resolution of our past is what we call healing.

It is essential to understand our suffering this way – as a reservoir of *unfinished* and *finished* emotional matter. For if we can visualize our past this way, we become aware of how it creates pain. Now, the challenge we face is to resolve our past experiences, while not creating new unresolved ones. This is the path of self-awareness, and it demands extraordinary focus and persistence.

Our goal is to ultimately answer the question, *"How do I heal from my suffering?"* We have already answered parts of this question as we studied our suffering in detail. However, we have not yet examined the "I" who suffers. To study this I require us to step into the realm of self-awareness.

NOTE:

There are three questions that arise out of this chapter which we are not yet equipped to answer.

They are:
1. How to not create new unresolved experiences that add to our past?
2. How to resolve our existing unresolved experiences?
3. What to do about experiences that can't be resolved?

Looking forward, the answer to the first question arises in Chapter 18: The Art of Seeing, the second in Chapter 19: Insight Meditation, and the third in the very last chapter. We will revisit these questions as the answers emerge. These three answers together bring about deep and irreversible healing. However, I caution you to be patient with this process.

Part of the reason why we find healing so difficult, is our eagerness to find answers. This eagerness leads us to accept superficial remedies such as positive thinking, attracting what we desire, manifesting our reality and so on. When these artificial solutions crumble, which they invariably do, we find ourselves right where we started. Therefore one of our main responsibilities is to cultivate patience while refusing to accept convenient or self-soothing answers. We have to insist on discovering what's real. Only then can we inspire authentic and profound shifts in ourselves. We have to be slow and deliberate in our search, and enjoy each step of the journey. We have to stop, look around and allow our minds and bodies to take it all in. So, let's keep exploring and see if the answers we seek arise from our self-inquiry.

Part 2

Finding Awareness

13
Self-awareness

We can't *think* about being clear and experience clarity, for thinking is the reason we are confused.

The word self-awareness is divided into two parts: self and the awareness of that self. That self includes everything from our thoughts, memories, fears, ambitions, desires and so on. Before we begin understanding what self-awareness can reveal about us, there is one question that we must clarify. That question is this: *"How can our mind be aware of itself, if it is in a state of chaos?"* For instance, if we are worried about losing our job, how can we observe ourselves in the middle of that fear? Wouldn't that fear prevent all self-awareness and self-observation? Can a fearful, anxious, or confused mind see its own situation objectively?

So then how do we begin? Our mind is already overwhelmed with fear, anxiety, desires, insecurity, and confusion. How can such a mind observe itself? How can it be self-aware? If we observe ourselves while experiencing these emotions all our observations are bound to be inaccurate. So if our mind has to observe itself it has to first become calm and relaxed. Otherwise, a disturbed mind observes itself and forms conclusions based on what it sees. This doesn't end the chaos, only furthers it.

Finding Awareness

Imagine a person being caught up in the current of a large and powerful river. Can such a person ever know where this river is headed? Can they see when the river goes over a fall, joins other rivers or meets the sea? Can they ever perceive this river in its full glory? They can't, because they are gasping for air, trying to stay afloat by hanging on to any driftwood they can find.

This river is the continuous stream of thoughts we experience everyday. It includes our mind chatter and all that goes along with it. It contains our unresolved memories, fears, desires, attachments, and so on. Its force and power come from our suffering. The more we have suffered, the stronger the current is. This river contains not just our personal history, but the history of our families and ancestors. It is our unconscious collective past flowing into the present. It's grip over us is absolute.

When we are in it, it creates a dream-like state. To become self-aware is to momentarily look at this river as a bystander – to open our eyes and step out of that dream. We can't observe this river unless we first pull ourselves out onto the banks. This means that our mind has to find a place of relative clarity, calmness and grounding such that it can observe itself. So the next question arises: *"How do I go about calming my mind?"*

What happens when we ask ourselves to calm down, or to not be afraid? We only get more agitated or scared, don't we? It seems impossible to create emotional states by wishing them into existence.

Forcing silence creates noise; forcing courage creates fear; forcing clarity creates more confusion. We can't think about being clear and experience clarity, for thinking is the reason we are confused. So then how can we observe the mind accurately?

One way to go about this, is by connecting with that part of us which doesn't think — our body. Our mind and body are deeply connected[8], yet in some ways they are separate. So, perhaps we can access the body and find the calmness that we need in order to begin observing ourselves. If we can tap into our bodies, then we may be able to find a state of calmness despite our agitated thoughts. This seems like a logical path forward.

As such, let's explore this mind-body connection more. Otherwise our attempts to save ourselves may be self-defeating. The river is powerful and our efforts to wade through the waters are feeble. This is why we have to find that tree on the riverbank, which is rooted into the earth. It's an object which is steady, grounded and centered. We must grip those roots and pull ourselves up onto dry land. Once we do that, we can anchor ourselves to this stationary vantage point and begin observing. We can rest in our bodies. There, we can find relative peace and quiet. Perhaps then we could observe this river of unconsciousness without being swept away in its flow.

---

8   The word 'mind' in this book is used to indicate only conscious and subconscious thought processes and emotions. It is not to be confused with the brain, which is the organ that controls our bodily functions. The brain, in that sense, is part of what I would call the 'body' in this book, because we can't exert any conscious control over the mechanisms the brain uses to control our heart rate, our muscles, or the functioning of the nervous, digestive or circulatory systems. A simple way to understand this is: mind equals conscious will and thinking; body equals unconscious physical functions and processes.

14
Finding the Bridge

The body reacts seamlessly to what the mind is seeing, regardless of whether it is real or imaginary.

Alex Honnold is a world-renowned professional climber. He is also one of the world's few free soloists. Free-soloing is a way of climbing mountains without ropes or any other gear. It requires a high degree of skill and physical fitness. It involves hanging on to steep and rugged rock faces with barely more than your fingernails and tip toes. It is as dangerous as it sounds. There is no room for even a small mistake. If you slip, you die.

In September 2008, Alex was free-soloing the half-dome of Yosemite Valley in California. Nine-tenths of the way up, at 2,000 feet off the ground, he had reached a narrow ridge on the mountain. True to its name, the Thank God Ledge varies from 5 to 12 inches in width and is only 12 meters in length. Walking across was the only way to reach the top for Alex. He made his way onto the narrow ledge and walked a few paces. Then he turned around and stood still with the mountain to his back and the valley to his front. Less than an inch in front of his toes lay the immensity of the valley and a vertical drop. This was not a time to

Finding Awareness

panic. There was no rope or harness to hold him, if he slipped. There was a chill in the air, but the wind was quiet. The sun was casting long shadows across the floor of the valley.

Then, as Alex was soaking in the exquisite beauty of the mountains, he did the unthinkable. He looked down towards his feet. As you read this, put yourself in Alex's shoes. Take a moment to visualize yourself 2,000 feet off the ground on one side of a rocky mountain face, standing on a ledge less than a foot wide, looking at the valley floor beneath you. Your toes are kissing the air. Just like Alex, you have nothing to hold on to. Then you look straight down. What do you feel?

Even if we imagine someone else's experience, we feel its effects on our mind and body. Our palms become clammy, our heart rate rises. Even imagining this from the comfort of our homes creates physical changes in the body. The more vivid our imagination is, the more details we see and the more fear we feel. This is the mind-body connection.

> The body reacts seamlessly to what the mind is seeing, regardless of whether it is real or imaginary.

This link between the mind and the body is so active that we even feel it during our sleep. This is why when we have a nightmare, we sometimes wake up with an increased heart rate and shortness of breath. Or if we take a fall in our dream, our whole body feels a jolt and we wake up, in what is known as a hypnic jerk. Our body can't always tell that the dream wasn't real. From its perspective, that nightmare or that fall, did happen. Our body responds to what our mind is witnessing, without questioning it.

Our mind, on the other hand, doesn't know any better either. If our physical self is under prolonged periods of stress, our mind feels anxious and worried too. If our heart rate is elevated, and it's not due to any physical activity, then it's a signal to the mind that something is wrong. It gets stressed. It's irrelevant to the mind that the heart rate increased

Finding the Bridge

because it was the mind that had imagined something dreadful in the first place! Tension in the mind becomes stress in the body. Stress in the body creates tension in the mind. *It's a two-way bridge.* Our mind and body are therefore prone to be caught in a vicious cycle reinforcing each other. They can create fear, stress, tension, worry, and anxiety out of thin air, if even one of them loses control.

This is why our anxiety and addiction are so difficult to manage. Every time we have an anxious thought, our body is already reacting to it. In return, our mind is responding to the changes in the body and becoming more anxious. As this cycle speeds up, our anxiety increases and spirals out of control. Similarly, if we are observing a compulsive desire, our body is already feeling the urge towards repeating a certain behavior. This physical urge instantly begins to feed the desire in our mind. This is why our effort to calm either the body or the mind seems futile. So, how do we proceed?

As we saw in the previous chapter, we turned to the body for a sense of grounding, because we witnessed that the mind was always in flux.

Now we discover that our body is in flux too because it shares a seamless connection with our mind.

This suggests that we can't consciously pull ourselves out of the river of unconscious thought, for we can neither affect the mind nor the body directly. They keep imbalancing each other, frustrating our efforts. Those of us who suffer from anxiety and crippling fears know this quite well. *We need access to something that is beyond our conscious will and therefore can't be affected by thinking. We need something which is always tethered to reality.*

Such a thing is our breath. Our breath is both in and out of our control. For instance, we can't hold it for a long time before our body takes over. Neither can we speed it up to a point and keep it there. We can exert only partial control over it. Then reality takes over. Breathing also regulates the two-way bridge between our mind and body. *This is why it is at the center of all meditation and self-awareness practices all across the world.* It is both directly related to the processes of life, and a tool to regulate the connection between our mind and the body. *It decides whether our thoughts can control our feelings.* This is why when we improve our breathing, it becomes possible to have an indirect and *simultaneous* influence over *both our mind and the body.* We will see how to do that in the next chapter.

Let's remember how we got here. Our original goal was to observe our mind. However, we can't do so because we are in the middle of our confusion. So we decided to find something that can't be confused, which is our body. But then, we discovered that our body is constantly influenced by our mind, so the body is confused too. The only way to proceed was to find something which is always (partially) beyond the control of thinking, which is our breath. Breath is the way we can disengage our mind from our body and allow the body to end its shared confusion. No matter how confused, afraid or anxious the mind gets, if we breathe right, we can keep our body calm and centered. We can keep it in touch with reality and begin to trust what it's saying. Now, we can pull ourselves out of that river. Breath shows the way.

NOTE:

In the next chapter, we will look at breathing in more detail and see how it can help us disengage and therefore harmonize both the mind and body. Breathing correctly can help us step out of our repetitive thought patterns and touch the present moment. From there, we can begin the process of Centering in our body. This process requires us to master three more arts. They are the art of hearing, seeing and feeling. Together, these four form the foundation of our self-awareness practice. If either of them is weak, so is our connection to reality. Only once we are centered, can we begin looking at our thoughts and understand what they reveal to us about *who we are*.

15
Walking the Bridge

The state of our mind is inseparable from the state of our breath.

How is your breathing at the moment? How's the state of your mind? You'll find that the answer to both these questions is one and the same. If our mind is calm, so is your breathing. If our mind is anxious, our breathing is shallow, rapid and uneven. If we are sad, our breath is characterized by short inhales and longer exhales. If we are in a state of dreamless sleep, our breathing is the deepest that it can be, because we are the most relaxed we can be.

If we have a shallow breathing habit, then our mind tends to create emotions that match those patterns. This is why poor breathing habits can make us feel tense all the time. We feel distressed without a cause. If we take a few conscious deep breaths, our mind begins to clear up and we feel calm. Just as poor breathing creates matching mental states, so does calm breathing.

Resonance frequency breathing

Why does this happen? The more even our breathing is, the more it regulates our heart rate. The more evenly our heart beats the more regulated we feel. The more regulated we feel, the more neutral and calm our emotions become. When our heart rate and breathing synchronize, our feelings and emotions begin to clear up. This frequency of breathing at which this happens is known as resonance frequency breathing. It tends to be five to seven breaths per minute for most people.[9] When we breathe at this rate, our moods begin to improve, and our stress levels begin to subside. Let's look at it a little deeper.

Before we proceed, a word of caution: All of us have a different body type, and therefore excessively controlling our breathing can cause some of us to experience hyperventilation or hypoxia (oxygen deprivation at a cellular level). The discomfort associated with breathing practices is also the primary reason why we stop practicing them. So the key is to find our rhythm without exerting a lot of influence over our breathing. We have to conserve effort. If it feels unpleasant, we have already overdone it. Breathing practices should always feel safe and natural.

There is a way to get to that five-to-seven-breaths-per-minute rhythm, without interfering with the natural ebb and flow of our breathing patterns. When our body wants to exhale, we exhale, except we exhale about ten percent more than we normally would. The physiological response to that exhalation will be a naturally deeper inhale. We allow it to happen. We stay with this rhythm for a while. If we feel comfortable, now we can add another ten percent to our exhalation. This will be followed by an even longer inhale cycle. This way, we continue breathing deeper until we get to between five and seven breaths per minute. We have now eased into a way of breathing which is deeper than what we are used to,

---
[9] When we breathe at this rate, we achieve the highest heart rate variability, a term which can be confusing. When it comes to HRV, the higher it is the better. High HRV is correlated with a lot of health benefits. A Practical Guide to Resonance Frequency Assessment for Heart Rate Variability Biofeedback, https://www.ncbi.nlm.nih.gov/pmc/articles/PMC7578229/

yet not so deep that it makes us feel uneasy. In doing so we have found our resonance frequency.

> In about 20 such breaths our mind begins to clear up and enter the present moment.

We have to experiment with this process to find the frequency that suits us, as it may differ with age and other factors. How do we know that we have found it? We feel a natural clearing of our thoughts and feel more upbeat than we usually do. We begin to feel more alert and active. Over time breathing this way can become a habit. Even if it doesn't, a few reminders everyday to correct our breathing go a long way in our emotional regulation. If the body chooses to go back to its habit of shallow breathing, we notice a change in our emotional state too. The more aware we become of this relationship between breath and emotions the more often we begin to regulate our breathing.

We also need to make sure that when we breathe, our lungs are expanding downwards, not upwards. That is, our diaphragm pushes downward and the belly moves out, instead of the shoulders moving up and down with each breath. This is called *diaphragmatic breathing*. We can practice this by placing your right hand gently on your belly, noticing its movement with each breath, while making sure that our shoulders stay in place. This way we get to a state of deep breathing without building up stress in our upper body. An impediment to belly breathing is our unconscious desire to hold our belly in, and chest out, such that it helps our appearance. As long as we are aware of this subconscious desire, we can find pockets of time in our day when we can practice our breathing without worrying about who may be watching us.

Centering

As we practice this method more and more, the space between our thoughts increases. We begin to perceive more of our immediate physical

Finding Awareness

surroundings. *We begin to leave our mind and center in our body*. Some of us feel new physical sensations, while others may start hearing new sounds. To some of us, colors of ordinary objects may seem brighter. As our mind becomes quieter, our conscious awareness effortlessly drops into our body.

> As long as we remain focused on breathing correctly, our emotional upheavals are unable to translate into physical ones.

This is the disengagement we were looking for in the previous chapter. Even if the mind is anxious, the body can now remain calm.

Once breathing this way becomes a habit, we naturally feel more interested in what our body sensations are telling us. We begin to trust our physical sensations and in doing so, transform our relationship with our own physical selves. Our mind still appears to be caught up in the flow of unconscious thinking, yet our body begins to seem like that tree deeply rooted into the earth. That earth is reality.

> NOTE:
> From here we can begin the process of centering further in our body. It has three parts to it. They are our senses of hearing, seeing, and feeling. *Only once we have fully centered ourselves, can we begin looking inwards at our thoughts, not before.* For me, when the breath deepens, hearing is the sense that intensifies first.

16
The Art of Listening

Total listening seamlessly transforms into total self-expression, because those who practice it are always flowing with the present moment.

This is an exchange that happened many years ago when I used to spend my evenings reading books, drinking coffee and meditating in a bookstore cafe. When you spend more than 20 hours every week in the same place you eventually become friends with folks who frequent it. He was in his twenties and had been working in the local company. We used to speak often and soon a friendship began to develop.

After a few days he told me about the difficulties he was facing in his new job. He seemed to have quite a dysfunctional relationship with his boss. He was working long days, and was getting paid half of what he deserved. He felt as if he wasn't valued. The constant criticism was affecting his self-esteem. Being an immigrant, he had signed a contract for one year. He was trapped. Just the thought of going to work was filling him with dread, and everyday our chats would end up in stories about what happened at his work. Eventually, I began to notice that even his voice would falter and trail off at the end of every sentence. When I asked him what was happening to his voice, he told me that his stress and anxiety were affecting his voice, he was literally unable to speak up.

When we would meet at the cafe, he would often look at the books I was reading. One day, I was reading a book on meditation. He asked me if perhaps meditation had a solution for someone like him. I told him perhaps it did, but he would have to do the work himself. He was willing to do anything to keep his sanity. After understanding his situation a little better, I told him that a solution to all his problems could be found in the art of listening, which we will discuss in this chapter. He was surprised but also curious. He had several questions about it, and we ended up speaking at length over a period of the next few days. Ultimately, he understood the essence of it and was ready to test these techniques at work. I didn't see him for a week after that conversation. Then one day, he came back to the cafe. He bought a cup of coffee, came over to my table and took a seat.

"I did what we had spoken about," he said.

The first thing I noticed was that his voice was deep and clear. He sounded confident. *"And what happened?"* I asked him.

"For the first three days, nothing changed. My interactions with him were as bad as they always were. On the fourth day, after trying really hard to listen, I zoned in. It was a strange feeling as if my brain had locked on to his voice. I couldn't hear anything else, just his voice. I couldn't perceive anyone else, just him," he said referring to his boss.

He continued, *"I found myself entering a space where I didn't have to consciously think before answering his questions anymore. The right answers, somehow, were just coming out of me. All I had to do was start talking and the precise thing that needed to be said would come out. I found it quite bizarre. Who was saying all this? Where were these answers coming from? Over the next three days, I noticed that I was beginning to lose the fear of interacting with him. As long as I practiced that particular way of listening, I felt no fear. My responses were fearless, appropriate, and creative. I could sense that my voice was not wavering either. Oh, and another thing happened. You know how I have always struggled with keeping my boundaries with him, right?"*

I nodded.

"When he tried it again this time, I just calmly said, 'Sorry, I won't be able to stay until 8 p.m today,' and waited for his response. I wasn't afraid at all. He seemed a little startled but then said, 'Ok, sounds good.' It was all over, just like that. All my problems with him seem to be gone within a week. I shouldn't get too excited, but I feel so empowered."

"What else happened?" I asked him.

"What is strange is that just one week ago, I despised this person, but now I don't. I am able to see why he has become the person he has. He once told me how he has relationship issues in his personal life. All he has going for him is his work. That's why he tries to control every aspect of it. In a strange way, I feel compassion for him. I am able to see where his words and actions are coming from, and I am able to look past them. Listening seems to be some kind of a superpower. For a moment, I felt as if I could read his mind!"

I could tell that my friend was excited with the way things had turned out, though these changes weren't that surprising. When we discover how to listen, dramatic changes begin to happen in our life. To experience them, we have to treat listening like an art form, or a skill and work on it slowly and patiently. Just like learning a musical instrument is a long-term project, so is developing our ability to listen. It is the first method of centering ourselves.

In order to know what listening is, let's see how it differs from hearing. Hearing and listening are similar, but they also have some important differences. Hearing is a passive activity and, as such, we rarely need any energy for it. Our brain hears all the time, even during sleep. Which is why light sleepers awaken even if there is a slight disturbance. Now, let's imagine that we were walking through a noisy marketplace. We can't hear anything in particular, just the humdrum of street life. But then, someone calls out your name. Instantly, the noise fades away and the name stands out. Why does this happen? This happens because the brain switches from passive hearing to active listening. It begins to pay attention when it picks up something of interest amidst all the noise that it keeps filtering out.

Conditioned listening

Now, even though our brain has switched from hearing to listening, it still has a long way to go in terms of how well it is capable of listening. This is because the kind of listening our brain practices first is *conditioned or divided listening*. The ordinary meaning of the word *listening* refers to this type. Let's look at the steps we go through in conditioned listening with an example.

Divided Listening:

1. We listen to their words.
2. We *analyze* their words and have an emotional response to them. Often, we are triggered.
3. Once the response is ready, we wait for the other person to stop speaking (or interrupt them).
4. Then we speak.

If the interaction was negative, we store it as an incomplete experience for further processing. *(This refers to unresolved emotional matter from Chapter 12 on Suffering)*

Let's look at this process with the help of an example:

- Someone says to us during a conversation, *"Why don't you think about this with an open mind?"*
- There is a surge of anger and hurt as we interpret what they said.
- We wait for them to stop talking so we can get back at them. If the hurt is deep, we even interrupt them.

- We blame someone else, then criticize and question their viewpoint.
- We remember this new hurtful conversation as it gets stored in our subconscious mind as unresolved content.

If you notice, in the above scenario in points 2 and 3, our attention slipped away from the act of listening. We got distracted and started processing our hurt, and remembering old memories, *while they were still talking*. In other words, we gave up active listening, and fell back into passive hearing. *This falling back happened when there was a surge of hurt that arose from our past.* Even though the example above is that of hurt coming up, desires or pleasures come up exactly the same way and interrupt our listening. Once this happens, everything we hear passes through a screen of past emotions.

As we saw in Chapter 12 on Suffering, our incomplete emotional past is always attempting to rise, and now it has entered our present conscious awareness. The pain from the subconscious mind has knocked on the door of our conscious mind, and has taken over our present. It has clouded our perception. Simply put, all of our past now stands between us and the people who we are talking to. *This is conditioned listening or listening through the past.*

Conditioned listening requires a lot less effort because we have all our judgments, prejudices, biases, insecurities, and fears eager to provide us answers. They make the decisions for us once they are evoked. When we prefer what our past has to say, over what the other person is saying in the present, we have begun reinforcing it. *This is why our relationships never seem to heal once they are broken.* How could they? Both people are engaged in conditioned listening, and therefore both their pasts are triggered and activated. They both see and hear each other through the filters that cloud their vision and mind. This is divided listening. It divides our attention into the past and the present.

> Conditioned or divided listening is one of the
> main reasons why our relationships do not heal,
> because it keeps reopening our old wounds.

Unconditioned listening

How does unconditioned or undivided listening look? It's fairly simple, in that we have to now train ourselves to listen with undivided attention. To try this out, listen to your favorite song with complete attention, with your eyes closed. Listen to every note, every instrument being played, every pause, every beat, every note, with an intention to not miss anything. When you do this, you will realize how much unnoticed beauty, subtlety and nuance there is even in those things we consider familiar. If we listen, we can discover hidden layers and meanings in those familiar sounds. *The deeper we go, the more there is to listen.* Our relationship with our loved ones is no different.

When we actively and intentionally listen to another person speak, a different world opens up. We begin to pick up on voice inflections, pauses and tones we had previously missed. When we combine listening with seeing (which we will discuss next), we notice the minutest facial movements and shifts in their body language. We notice the spaces between their thoughts, the hidden fears and desires betrayed by their words. Their voice gives away what's *truly* on their minds. We begin to perceive the emotional states from which they speak and are able to touch the heart of who they are as human beings.

This in no way means that we presume we know more about what they are thinking than them, but only that we are fully present and available to them. We feel a profound compassion for them. If we listen this way, we can never violate the freedoms of another, for we are listening with care, attention and love. So, how does this undivided way of listening compare with what we saw earlier?

Undivided listening:

1. We begin to listen to their words.
2. We focus all our mental resources on listening and create a state of complete concentration. We converge on their voice.
3. We disregard any urge to interpret, process or analyze and stick to active listening.
4. We allow a response to emerge and speak when the time is right.
5. We finish the experience leaving behind no *unprocessed* emotional pain, hurt or pleasure. There is nothing more left to be said, for we have said it already. The conversation is over.

Here is an example:

- They say, *"Why don't you think about this with an open mind?"*
- All our focus is only on their voice and nothing else. Our concentration is absolute.
- We feel our emotions awaken, but continue following the sound of their voice, and *not* our emotions. We register what they say later, such as, *"I think this will help you, I say it only with the best of intentions."*
- A calm center generates a spontaneous and appropriate response, *"I will think about it."*
- Our response is wholesome and effective. We feel resolved at the end of every interaction.

This is undivided listening. *It feels like an unbroken flow of attention from start to finish*. Here, in point 2 and 3, we listened to their words, instead of activating our past hurt or pleasures. That is why we actually heard what they had to say – that they didn't mean to hurt us, but said whatever they did perhaps out of care. Now, we can't be angry because we understand them. We don't get hurt either. Even if they *did* intend to hurt us, they wouldn't be able to, for *we would see the place where that hurt is coming from, taking away its power*. We would still let them express themselves.

This doesn't mean that we always allow others to talk over us. Why? Because our response is never planned. It is spontaneous. If the moment dictates as such, we interrupt them too. Whatever our response is, it always arises from the depths of the present moment. When we listen with every bit of energy we have, we instinctively know what to say and do. *We let the situation decide what's right or wrong, not our unresolved past. That's why our action doesn't come from a place of anger or weakness, but from a place of calmness and power.*

Total listening seamlessly transforms into total self-expression, because those who practice it are always flowing with the present moment.

The source of our answers

As we said in the beginning, this is an art. Undivided listening is a trainable skill. It is a way to listen with our subconscious or the deep mind. This is why, in step 3, it's important that we continue to listen, while letting go of the desire to process and formulate a response. The only way to experience this is to try it. When we practice undivided listening, our responses come from a place of *true integrity* to who we are human beings, therefore they never disappoint us.

If we listen this way, we are often surprised at the things we say when it's our turn to speak, just as my friend did. This is so because the response of the subconscious mind is always intuitive, sensitive, proportioned and appropriate. Even though (as we have seen in earlier chapters) the subconscious contains unprocessed pain, it also contains the truth of who we are as human beings. It contains all our history, and therefore our potential.

Our subconscious mind knows the correct responses to any given situation. We just need a method to untangle them from our unresolved hurts. Listening intently seems to be one way to do it. It deactivates our unresolved past, and empowers our deepest inspirations. It acts in the moment. Since all of us have a different past, there is no one correct response to any given situation. The perfect answer is *whatever each one of us thinks and does in that particular moment,* as long as we are listening with undivided attention.

If we listen this way we are able to give all the space available, to the other person and their words, while enabling our true selves to exist. We not only honor their presence, but also honor our own reality.

NOTE:

As outlined in the previous chapter, our intent is to learn how to connect with our bodies, for they are a conduit of reality itself. Even though what we listen to is outside of us, undivided listening takes us deep within the mind and connects us with ourselves. This art of listening can be practiced not just in our relationships, but also during times of solitude – during meditation. Then we start connecting with the ordinary reality of the present moment. We can hear that slow hum of the air conditioner in our room, the cars passing by on the street, the leaves of a tree rustling in the wind, the dog barking in the distance, the children playing, or the bird tweeting a morning song. As our mind becomes still, our attention deepens further. We can hear our breath and its serenity. We can hear the steady beating of our hearts even without taking a pulse. We are here, in our bodies, and connecting with it for the very first time.

17
The Art of Feeling

Our mind is rarely as close to reality, as is our body.

I must have been 10 years old when I first saw the movie *Enter the Dragon*. In the first few scenes, Bruce Lee's character is teaching martial arts to a young student. When he asks the student a question about using intuition, the kid says, *"Let me think."* Bruce knocks him on the head and says, *"Don't think, feel. It's like a finger pointing at the moon. If you concentrate on the finger, you'll miss all the heavenly glory."*

As a child, who could watch martial arts movies all day, I was quite moved by that statement although I didn't understand why. I felt that there was something interesting that he just said and left it at that. I only understood what he meant 20 years later, when my martial arts teacher demonstrated the same principle to me in a different way.

He had me stand in front of him. Then he raised up his hand, to his shoulder level, and held a $1 bill, lightly between his index and thumb finger. With the hand facing towards the floor, he said, *"I am going to release this bill and it's going to float to the ground like a feather. You have to catch it with your thumb and index finger, the same way I am holding it. There is only one condition. You can't move your hand from this position."*

Finding Awareness

He brought my hand right where the bill was and arranged it for a pincer grasp, as he prepared to release the bill. My hand was merely an inch away from the top of the bill, where he was holding it. My index finger was behind the bill, and the thumb in front of it, ready to catch. All I had to do was pinch at the right moment, and I would catch it. I waited for him to release it. This was going to be so easy.

"*Ready?*" he said and let go of the bill. Instantly, I pinched my index and thumb together, hoping to catch it. I failed, and it gently floated to the ground.

"*Try again.*" He did the same thing. I failed again. He did this five times, then asked me, "*Do you know why you are not able to catch it?*"

I shrugged. I had no idea why this simple task seemed so hard.

He said, "*Because right now, you are caught up in thinking. You aren't feeling. Feeling is everything.*"

"*But how?*" I asked him.

Then he took my left hand and had me touch the forearm of the hand holding the bill in.

He said, "*Now feel for the sensations in my arm when I release the bill.*" As he dropped it this time, I was able to easily catch it. My left hand could sense the movement of his muscles, and I could respond instantly with my right hand to catch the bill. I didn't have to think. The time it took for me to see and respond, was much longer than it took me to feel and respond to the same challenge. *Feeling was ahead of thinking. It was already there.*

Then he asked me to close my eyes and repeat the exercise. Every time he let go of the bill, I caught it, even with my eyes closed.

He said, "*You see, when you put a distance between yourself and reality, you can't meet up with it. You can't respond to it in real time. With no connection to my hand, you have no idea what is happening. But when you can stay connected with me, you can move with me, you can feel, and you can respond. You are present, aware and you are able to act without thinking.*"

The Art of Feeling

The martial arts aspect of that lesson was to develop sensitivity to your opponent's movements, but in my mind I was already drawing parallels to how our mind works. When we are disconnected from our physical reality, we create a mental reality in order to understand it. The time we don't spend in our bodies, we spend in our minds. There is only one place our conscious attention can be at a time – either the present or the past.

---
*The present is the feeling, the past is the mind.
There is no in between.*

We alluded a little to this distance from reality, and how to reduce it, when we looked at our ability to *listen* in the previous chapter. Listening is the first method of centering, while feeling is the second. Just as undivided listening reduces the space between us and other people, so does *feeling* reduce the space between us and our physical reality. If that space exists, it is quickly filled up by our thoughts. This staying *in touch* with our physical sensations requires a retraining of our mind.

It requires unconditioning the habitual relapsing into mental narratives at least a few times a day and simply noticing what sensations one is feeling at any given time. The best way to experience this is to actually do it. The next few paragraphs are a guided meditation in developing sensitivity to our physical sensations. It will take us through both inner and outer body awareness. This meditation is designed to bring you out of your mind and into your body.

In order to begin this meditation, prepare yourself by taking 20 conscious breaths at the rate which you decided was right for you, in the chapter on breathing. This is usually five to seven breaths per minute. This will clear up any mental fogs you are in. Once that is done, spend about a few minutes intently listening to the sounds around you, and connecting with your sense of hearing. Get to the point where we were at the end of the last chapter – that is being able to *hear* or feel your heartbeats. If you feel uncomfortable or uneasy, please skip the meditation and read on. Otherwise, find your heartbeat before you proceed.

119

Finding Awareness

~ Guided Meditation Begins ~

- As you pay attention to your heartbeat, feel the pulse travel through your entire body, like a ripple in the pond, moving outwards, towards your fingertips and toes. Take a deep breath and focus on the tingling sensations in the fingertips of both your hands.

- Stay here for a few seconds and gradually move your attention up from your fingertips to our wrists. Gently open and close your palms, and slowly rotate your wrists. Can you feel every joint in each finger as you close your palms? Remember each sensation. Feel every movement. Now, slowly move your attention further up to your elbows. Can you feel your elbows, without moving or touching them? Ask yourself if you're sensitive enough to feel your elbows, without moving them.

- Stay here as long as you need to, as your conscious mind *remembers* your elbows and slowly finds the sensations in them. Then move up to your shoulders. Pay attention to the weight they are carrying. Relax and take a deep breath. Now move your attention to your neck. Tuck your chin back and lift up the top of your head as if it's suspended from a string above your head. Take a few breaths and feel the stress in your neck dissolve. Let it drop towards your shoulders and down your arms to your fingertips. Let it go. Take a deep breath and acquaint yourself with this safety within. Say, *"I will always be safe in here."*

The Art of Feeling

- Now move your attention to your face. Can you *feel* your chin without touching it? As you wait for the sensations to come back, feel the facial muscles begin to relax. Scan your jaw, your nose, your eyelids then your forehead for sensations. Take a deep breath. Can you feel your eyebrows, without touching them? Can you let go of the stress they carry? Now gently move your attention to your forehead. Here, rest your attention and feel the lightness begin to spread through your face. Take a deep breath and acquaint yourself with this safety within. Say, *"I will always be safe in here."*

- Now slowly move your attention down to your spine towards your back. Gently move our shoulders back so that your chest feels open and the back feels straight. Feel your torso hang on your spine, like a coat rests on a hanger. Let all the stress seamlessly move downwards and into the ground. Take a deep breath and acquaint yourself with this safety within. Say, *"I will always be safe in here."*

- Now take a deep breath and scan all the sensations you feel in your chest. Traverse down to your navel. Feel the gentle movement of your belly like a rise and fall of the tide with each breath. As you do this, see whether you can feel the inside of your belly. Connect with your sense of hunger. Remember how hunger feels. Stay a moment here. Your entire upper body should feel as if it is brimming with sensations. Take a deep breath and acquaint yourself with this safety within. Say, *"I will always be safe in here." (continued)*

- Now slowly drop your attention into your legs. Can you feel your hamstrings without touching or moving them? Take a deep breath and *search* for those sensations. Now, can you feel your calves and thighs? How about your knees? Spend as much time as you need looking for these forgotten parts of your body. Respect them, get to know them. They are you. Now move attention to your ankles, the joint you have perhaps ignored for years. They have been carrying your weight without complaining since you could first walk. Can you feel how strong they are? Take a deep breath and acquaint yourself with this safety within. Say, *"I will always be safe in here."*

- Now bring your attention to the toes of your right foot. Can you *feel* your third toe without moving or touching it? How about the fourth? Take as long as you need to, and *remember* each and every one of your toes individually. Once you are done noticing the sensations in them, see whether you can *feel* your entire body from head to toe. Take a deep breath and feel it all at once. Take a deep breath and acquaint yourself with this safety within. Say, *"I will always be safe in here, because this is my home."*

~Meditation Ends~

This requires us to become aware of everything happening inside and outside of our bodies. Conscious feeling teaches us that it's possible to find a safe home within ourselves. We are not judging our feelings, but simply paying attention to them. Now we can look at one of the most undervalued and important senses we have, the sense of *sight*. Let's look at the art of seeing in more detail.

18
The Art of Seeing

Seeing one thing properly, is worth more than seeing a hundred things superficially.

One of the memorable times of my life was when I visited the Yellowstone National Park in Wyoming. Situated on a volcanic caldera is one of the most diverse ecosystems on the planet. Needless to say, everything one sees here from the mesmerizing colors forming in the hot springs, to the rolling hills, to the bison, the bears and even the occasional wolf is unparalleled in its beauty. One day, we were sitting alongside a lake in the early hours of the morning.

The mist was rising up from the lake and a lone bison was grazing in marshes nearby. The sun was beginning to rise, as the mallards were coming out to feed. Meanwhile, a couple of cars came by and parked near our spot. A few people got out, held up their binoculars and stared peering at everything. One of them had a big camera hanging from his neck. Some others were taking pictures from their cellphones. Just as this was happening, a bald eagle came and perched himself on a leafless branch of a dead pine tree about 50 meters away from us.

Finding Awareness

As this happened, the photographer of the group took note of it. He quietly put up his tripod and began taking pictures. The bald eagle waited, and so did he. Something moved on the surface of the lake. The eagle leaned forward with its eyes locked onto a target. Then it swiftly descended from its branch, swooped down and tried to grab a fish in its claws. It missed, flew around, and perched itself on the same spot again. Everything was perfectly quiet and whole. Then it happened.

"Ok everyone, let's get back in the car. We are running late, there is more to see here," complained someone in their group. The photographer was annoyed by this jarring interference and refused to leave. He wanted to be left behind. After nudging him a few more times, the rest of this group got inside their cars and hurried away. Only one observer remained. After 10 minutes, the eagle left its branch again and drifted towards its prey. As it neared, it skimmed the surface creating a small wave behind it. Then it grabbed a fish and disappeared into the fog. The photographer took a few pictures. Then he stepped away from his camera and soaked in the beauty of the lake, the fog, and the sunrise. He was in no hurry.

He was left behind with the slowness of the present, while the rest of his crew rushed towards a future that was yet to pass. He witnessed what was in front of him, while they were absorbed in their own imagination. He experienced, while they expected and imagined. He observed, while others verbalized. He wanted to see what was in front of him, the rest only saw what their minds were showing them.

Why do we lose sight of what's in front of us? We are no strangers to undivided seeing, are we? We too have engaged in complete witnessing of an event, such as a sunset, or our children playing etc., yet at some point we *fall out* of seeing. This *falling out of the present* has to be understood if we are to understand seeing. Let's examine this with the help of a Zen story.

A Zen koan

There was once a zen teacher and his three disciples who went on a morning walk around their village. As they came upon the edge of the forest the teacher stopped and pointed towards a shrub. A sole red flower was growing on top of a thin branch. He took his disciples towards it and asked the first one, *"What do you see?"*, while pointing at the flower.

The first student said, *"I see the past I left behind to become a monk. I once gave such a flower to a girl I was in love with many years ago."*

The teacher then turned to the second student, *"What do you see?"*

The second monk said, *"What a beautiful flower. Perhaps we can offer it at the shrine of the Buddha. Should we take it?"*

Then he pointed at the oldest of the three disciples, *"And you, what do you see?"*

"I see the symbol of enlightenment."

At which the teacher began laughing uproariously and started to walk on. Just as this happened, a small girl from the village came to the spot, plucked the flower, put it in her basket and walked away. *"There goes your enlightenment,"* said the teacher and they continued on their path.

This koan, just as many others, is inconclusive, though it reveals the way we engage in the act of seeing. The first student couldn't see the flower because of his unresolved past. It was triggered in the form of hurt and took over his present experience. The second student too, had his past reappear, though in the form of unresolved pleasure. He wanted to re-experience the familiar comfort of his rituals. The third student was caught up in conceptual (over) thinking. Let's look at these ways and see what they reveal about the way we see.

As we saw in Chapter 12 on suffering, our unresolved emotional past is always trying to find completion. It is looking for an opening into our conscious mind. It gets that opportunity when we come across a person, event or a situation that reminds us of our past. When it arose in the mind of the first monk, he stopped seeing the flower, and became trapped in his memories. When such a thing happens to any of us, a powerful hallucination begins. We begin to daydream. If someone were to look at our face at this time, they would see that our eyes have zoned out. Sometimes we appear cross-eyed, as if we are not there at all. We are lost in thought. Our body may be here, but our mind is reliving some distant memory.

This disconnection with reality also happens when unresolved pleasure (or fear) is triggered. Rushing about trying to get to the next scenic view out of fear of missing out, or the pleasure of making a ritual offering, removes us from the present moment in the same way. We see an alternate reality. Our past splits our attention into half. One half is trying to be here, while the other half is trying to desire (or escape) what doesn't exist. In the process we forget to see what's in front of us.

Sometimes, we have a hyper-active imagination and get caught up in overthinking. Just like the third monk, we start thinking about a concept, an idea we consider to be of great urgency. This tendency to conceptualize also appears to be a symptom of our fears and desires. The monk was afraid of not achieving the state of enlightenment, as much as he yearned for it. His mind was obsessed with it so that's what he saw. The teacher laughed because he laid a trap for his students, which they all fell into. The point was perhaps just to see the flower move in the wind, or to see an eagle catch its prey, without any self-seeking.

These impediments to seeing – unresolved hurt, fear and desires– are always active. As such, we are never truly seeing anything without their shadow. For instance, how often can we sit quietly in the woods and see nothing but the trees? How often do we pick up a stone and examine it closely, not looking for anything in particular, but just seeing its simplicity and quietness, like a child would? How often do we look at the people we love, as if we are seeing them for the first time? How often have we looked at another human being, without judging, projecting or expecting a single thing from them?

We can't see this way because we are always seeing through our past conditioning. It forms a veil in front of our eyes and clouds our vision. This conditioning takes the form of routine or normalcy. For example, when we walk down the street that we live on, there is always this sense of familiarity that creeps in. Notice how our mind immediately becomes dull to the aliveness of the street. We have walked it a thousand times so how could there be anything new to see? We abandon conscious seeing and slip into conditioned seeing. When we are taking a walk outside, our body is physically there, but our mind is more or less absent. It's walking down an entirely different and non-existent street in a world of its own making.

Undivided seeing

What happens if we can, even if for a few minutes, let go of all the layers of memories and emotions, and see something without the film of the past blocking it? What happens when we go for a walk with a clean, new mind?

When I first walked with this intention, I discovered that there was a gentle slope in the road I used to run on. I realized why I always seemed to prefer running the opposite way; it must've felt easier to run down the slope. As the road took a turn, I noticed there was a large magnolia tree at the corner, hiding in plain sight. Now I knew why the air smelled like honey and lemons in the spring. When I walked further down, I passed my friend's house. His cat was sitting outside by the gate. As I walked by, it came towards me to greet me. I reached down to pet it, and for the first time I noticed that one of its eyes was green, while the other was azure blue. Further down the road, I saw a large beehive on a tree – surely a worrisome sign for the house underneath it. Then I came upon the traffic light. When it turned green, I looked at it longer than I ever had. It appeared to be much brighter than usual, I felt as if I could have looked

Finding Awareness

at it for hours. This was a strange and new layer of reality, underneath the ordinary one. It was rich, beautiful and deeply fulfilling, just as it was.

To truly *see* is to find a new world within the old, to feel an unfamiliarity underneath the familiarity. Stop reading this book for a minute and just look around you. Look for things you haven't seen before wherever you are sitting. Find out what has been hiding in plain sight. Whether you are outdoors, or indoors, even inside our own bedroom, you can see new things that you haven't before.

> A good meditation practice is to see something new in your meditation room everyday, however insignificant.

Look at the chair resting on the floor, the table next to it, and the coffee cup on the table. Look at the book besides it, its cover, its pages, how much of it has been read. Look at that pair of glasses, that table lamp, and the wire that connects it to the wall. Follow the wall to the ceiling, look at the fan hanging from the ceiling, look at the opposite wall, and down to the floor again. Look at the small marks and dents in its color and texture. Notice how it reflects the light. Look at your own hands. Turn them over, look at the backside of your palms, your knuckles, your mid-knuckles, your nails and the tips of your fingers. Have you ever seen your own body properly? Look at your fingernails in detail, your palms and the lines on them, the tiny grooves that make up your fingerprints. Notice how alive the hands feel when you examine them closely. Notice the color, the shape and size of everything around you – the forms different things take.

Seeing with intention is the third way of centering. To cultivate *seeing*, like *hearing* and *feeling*, takes a lot of intention, focus and also rest. Our aim is not to strain ourselves by trying to see, hear and feel, but to become more sensitive to our physical reality. It forms the basis of our inward connection to ourselves. When our body awareness is deep, it helps us find safety in the present moment, regardless of our outward circumstances.

We began this section of the book by consciously developing our breathing. Once we were in our bodies, we intensified our *listening, feeling* and *seeing*, all of which are meditations in themselves. *To hear only with our ears, to feel only with our body, and to see only with our eyes brings us closer to our unique and ever changing reality.* If we can't practice all of these at once, it's enough to practice each one of them just once, for seeing one thing profoundly is worth more than seeing a thousand things superficially. Often, one moment of clarity is all that is needed to spark an irreversible change in ourselves.

> NOTE:
>
> We have now answered the first of the three open questions from the end of chapter 12: *How to not create new unresolved experiences that add to our past?* We have witnessed how undivided listening, feeling and seeing help us create resolved and finished experiences. When we are fully centered, our response to any life situation is instant and exhaustive. When we laugh, we laugh freely, when we cry, we give in, when we speak, we speak precisely, and when we love, we love passionately. We meet life without holding back. *This totality of centered experiencing prevents new unresolved memories from being created. We solve our problems as they are arising, instead of postponing them, because all our mental*

faculties are available to us, here and now. There may still be some problems that need to be solved at a later time, though our decision to postpone them is conscious and measured.

If we practice these methods of centering, we can make our body aware of our mind, whereas we have always known our mind to be aware of our body. Fluctuations in our body (such as changes in breathing or heart rate) can alert us of our mind becoming caught up in an emotional storm. We have always considered our body to be secondary and mind to be primary. Now, we have reversed that relationship and restored our inward balance. What our body perceives through these various channels is now primary and what our mind chatter says is secondary. In other words, we have stepped out of that river of conditioned thinking we saw in Chapter 13, and have anchored ourselves to the earth. We can trust our body to show us the way forward. We are prepared to observe that vast river of human consciousness flowing through us. We can now begin to learn the Art of Observing our thoughts.

19
The Art of Observing

Insight meditation is the art of understanding a question in a different way, and discovering that this new way of looking at the question itself is its answer.

We have taken a long journey to arrive here. Until now we have avoided a direct observation of our thoughts. Though now, we are centered in our body. We have trained ourselves to breathe, listen, feel and see deeper. Unbeknownst to us, this process of centering has sharpened our senses. We have become sensitive to our physical sensations. In doing so we have cultivated a space which is free of thoughts. This space is why thought-awareness has now become possible.

We will go about this by picking up one problem and unraveling it. Through this observation our goal would be to understand the problem, not to resolve it. We will examine it without nudging it in any preconceived direction. We are going to find out if it's possible to understand our deepest problems and become self-reliant. This self-reliance makes us more powerful, for we begin to trust that the solutions to our problems are within our grasp. We think of our minds as being too complex and therefore avoid looking within. We prefer to lean on someone else to solve our problems. This chapter is meant to challenge that assumption. We're not saying that consulting experts is unnecessary, but perhaps we are capable of doing more than we think.

This is a system, a method of self-inquiry which both has, and is free of specific rules. It's a method which we can learn and have insights into our own specific problems. This is the heart of meditation – the art of perceiving what is happening within, without distortion. Let's look at two specific problems, and see how they unravel when we observe them. These are two of the conversations I have had with my readers on Insight meditation.

Conversation 1

"I was recently in a relationship. It ended abruptly and I am in a lot of pain. I feel lonely. Can you help me understand this problem using insight meditation? How do I rise out of this situation?"

"Alright, let's look at this carefully. You said you wanted to rise out of this situation. What do we mean by rising out?"

"Hmm. I don't quite know. I think I want to move on. But I don't know how. I keep getting these thoughts about our past and I remember all the good times, and the bad times. I also feel so lonely now that I am not with him. I remember everything and it's hurting me at the moment. I want to move on."

"Let's see if we can slow our thinking down a little. When we have to go deep into a problem, we have to take each aspect of it individually. We can't look at everything at once. We can't look at the memories, the loneliness, and the moving on together, you see? If you notice, there are three different problems. We'll pick one and go deeper into it, okay?"

"I guess you're right. It is all so overwhelming. I am not able to keep one thing in my mind."

"Remember to breathe. Take a few deep breaths and pay attention to your body. Once you feel a little clear, pick up one of these problems. Remember to take your time. There is no rush. There is no deadline to solve anything. We have all the time in the world. Breathe, relax and, when you feel comfortable, pick one."

"I understand. I want to take the problem of moving on. How do I move out of this mental space?"

"What do we mean by the words moving on? What do we mean when we say I want to move on from this situation? How do we define moving on?"

"I think I want to feel better. I want to heal."

"So, you don't want to feel all this pain? Is that right?"

"Yes, I don't want to feel this pain."

"If that's the case, we have to look at where the pain is coming from, right? Where does it come from?"

"From the memories?"

"Right, so the pain is in the memories, but I don't want my memories. I don't want to remember anything. Let's say, if there was a switch I could flip, I would flip it and erase everything, right? Is that what you want, to erase every memory of this person?"

"No! I don't want to forget him. I guess, I just don't want to remember the bad things that happened. I want to remember the good times, and forget the bad ones." As she said this, she paused a little, then continued. "Okay, I see what you mean. I am selectively trying to let go of the pain, while remembering all that was good."

"Which means that there is an internal conflict going on, right? If we have to be honest with ourselves, we don't want to forget anything at all. We just want our life to go back to the way it was – happy and blissful, right? We *just want the pain to leave, without touching anything else. Don't say yes or no right away. Take a minute to examine it."*

She did. After a minute, she nodded in agreement.

"So, look what has happened. We started off by saying that we want to move on, but now we are discovering that we don't want to move on after all. If anything, we want to go back in time to the way things were. We are mourning the loss of what we had. Would you agree?"

"Yes. I see it. I feel a little better. But I can't explain why."

"Remember this feeling. We feel better because now we are admitting the reality of what is. We had an insight, and it moved us from denial into acceptance. This acceptance brought an end to the conflict between this idea of moving on, and the reality of not wanting to. But let's not stop here. Let's keep looking. So we see that we want to go back in time, yet, things are not going to go back to normal, right? Too much has happened. Now we are alone and hurt. So, what do we do now?"

"Yes, that's correct. My relationship can't go back to how it was. I can't reverse time. But I don't want to be stuck here forever either. I want to keep moving forward but the memories just keep coming. What should I do when I go back to living my daily life and this pain comes back?"

"Okay, now let's understand this pain. How do we define it? What do we mean, exactly, when we say I am feeling hurt, or I am feeling pain?"

"I think the way I would define it is…"

I interrupted her.

"Don't define pain. Tell me how you're feeling. We aren't really looking for theoretical definitions, you see. We are asking ourselves how do we perceive our own pain, you understand? Sorry to interrupt you, but it's important that when we undertake Insight meditation, we correct our course before we go down the wrong path. Please continue."

She continued, *"Yes, I understand. I think it's just a lot of memories. I remember an incident, and the words that he and I said, and I feel pain. I am feeling that pain as I speak to you,"* she said wiping her eyes.

"So, our memories contain the emotional pain. When we touch those memories, the pain they contain overflows into the present. Do you see? We feel it all over again. The past becomes alive and we begin to relive it, right?"

"Yes, I see it. But then are you suggesting that I block those memories so that I don't feel the pain?"

"Let's go even slower. What will happen if we block those memories from coming up? Observe it. Take your time. I see that my memories cause pain when I remember them. Does it mean I should block my memories? What will happen if I block my memories?"

"Okay, I follow what you're saying," she said with a renewed intention.

I said, "Superficially, it seems true that if we don't remember our past we won't feel the pain, yet if we block our past, what happens? Does the past go away? If we distract ourselves, think positive thoughts or lose ourselves in substances? Is forgetting the same as healing?"

"No, forgetting is definitely not healing. If I force myself to forget I just remember more, or worse, I feel bottled up. It builds up inside me and then it comes out all at once. I also start drinking to forget, which is another problem."

"Exactly right. Avoiding or blocking away our memories from arising can't help us in the long run. It usually backfires. Let's remember why these painful memories arise in the first place. They are trying to resolve themselves. You and your partner both walked away with hurt. You both have unsaid things. There is a lot of regret, fear, anger and guilt. All of that turned into unprocessed hurt, right?"

"Yes, I remember this from our previous conversations. The past is arising because of the unprocessed emotional content in our memories. Our rising past *is nothing but our memories and emotions trying to finish what we started. I remember you had said that our subconscious mind doesn't like to store any unfinished business. It keeps trying to resolve those issues and that creates painful thoughts,"* she said.

"Right, and this happens in the form of flashbacks. Do you see all of this clearly?"

"Yes, I see it."

"Let's recap what we have discovered so far. Our past creates pain. We can't stop this pain otherwise it may get bottled up and lead to other problems. This pain is arising on its own and trying to resolve an old hurt. If we resist it, we create another problem on top of an existing one. Would you agree?"

She nodded. *"It seems as though I can't fight the past. So wait a minute. Does that mean I should just give up and let it consume me?"* she asked.

"Glad you asked, because that's our next question. Let's say I have a flashback and I see an old conversation happening again. I feel the pain rising. Now I know I can't fight it, otherwise it gets bottled up, so what will happen if I let it take me?"

She replied, *"It will cause a lot of pain and it's kind of like wallowing in pain. There is no control over it. It will do whatever it wants. There may be no end to it. I have had episodes where I will get lost in a memory and spend hours and hours in that state. When I finally come back to the present, I realize that I wasted so much time and energy in it. Giving up like that makes me miserable."*

"Right. Are you saying that we can neither fight the pain, nor let it win?" I asked her.

"Yes. That's how it seems to be. I can't suppress it, neither can I let myself be lost in pain. So, what do I do?"

"You tell me," I said, "What remains? If you can't say yes and you can't say no, then what do you say?"

She took a long pause.

"You don't say anything. You remain quiet."

"That's right. Remaining quiet. Which means when the pain arises, letting it arise without interfering with it. It won't be easy, because the pull of past memories is quite strong. The pain wants you to get involved in it somehow. Even if you touch it, it will grab hold of you and pull you in."

"How do I prevent myself from getting pulled in?" she asked.

"You know what another word for such quietness is?" I asked her.

She shook her head.

"Awareness. That's another word for being quiet. When we reject our thoughts, we bottle them up. When we indulge in them, we become miserable. When we neither condemn nor justify, we remain quiet. We are just aware of what is happening, right?"

"I see what you mean. It seems like a tightrope walk."

"It is, but with a slight difference. Here, it's okay to fall. The important thing is to get back up and allow this process of release to go on uninterrupted. To keep getting up on that tightrope and making sure we are not fighting or fueling our pain. When all our subconscious pain is done rising and leaving, it leaves us cleansed. We are not forgetting the past, but letting it be. That is what it means to heal."

"This seems so hard to do! You are asking too much of me."

"I am not asking anything of you. I am going where our inquiry is taking us."

"That's true. But my mental dialogue begins even before I make a choice. I wake up in the morning, and I am already talking about my ex. How do you expect me to be quiet, when I don't know or can't tell when I began to talk? How can I not justify or condemn my past when I am already doing so as I wake up?"

Finding Awareness

"This is good. That is our next question. Let's look at it. As we said earlier, the past arises in the form of images and visuals, right? It also arises in the form of words. You'll find yourself entertaining old arguments, role-playing with yourself as your ex. It all happens in the mind as it keeps unearthing the remnants of the past, recreating those emotions and pain. To be aware, and quiet is to simply ride this tide as best as you can. All we have to do is be aware that we are going through a period of suffering, and let it happen without rushing or slowing the process. Just say to yourself, 'This is the past leaving', and it will help you release it with patience and dignity."

"So it is important to be aware as I suffer through it. Simply by being there when the pain arises and being quiet. Letting the mental dialogue play itself out while remembering, and reminding myself to just stay aware through it all. If I get pulled in, then without judging myself, taking a deep breath, re-aligning myself and carrying on."

"That is all."

"This is the past leaving. This is the past leaving. This is the past leaving," she chanted as we ended our conversation.

Conversation 2

"I am triggered very easily by my partner. We have many arguments because of my temper. For many years, I had no awareness of this, but when I started practicing self-awareness, I became a little more aware of my insecurities and fears. I began to realize that there are times when I lost control over myself, became too angry, and that led to fights. How do I control my anger?"

"Sure, do you want to go into anger?"

"Yes, I want to learn how to control my anger."

"Let's start with examining our existing definitions of the problem we are trying to examine. Often this is the simplest way inward. So, what do you mean by that word, anger? How would you describe it, without using the word?"

"I guess I am angry, when I lose my temper?"

"Right, but what happens when you lose your temper? Go into it."

"I think I lose control when I lose my temper."

"That's right. Now if you lose control when you get angry, wouldn't that mean you had control before it? Just by extension of logic. You had control, and then you lost it, right?"

"Yes, seems reasonable. I think that's right. I lose control."

"So, what is control?"

He began laughing a little nervously. He felt trapped. I could tell he was getting uneasy.

"I am feeling quite nervous. This feels weird."

"Yes, it does, because we have not learned how to focus our attention. How to have a laser-like focus while observing the mind. Every time I do this with someone it gets intense and some people feel unpleasant. But this is what meditation requires. A determination to see it through to the very end. Take a deep breath. This is an exploration. Relax and see how it goes. See what comes up. Even I don't know where this leads. I am discovering with you too. Let's explore and see what happens. Let's enjoy this."

"Okay," he said as he exhaled deeply. He closed his eyes for a few seconds. He was centering and grounding to his sensations, the most important part of any meditation. Then he spoke.

"I think to have control is to be in charge of your life, of your thoughts. It is to feel like you can do whatever you want in the present moment."

"That's right. Control is the ability to do what you want in the present, right? So what did anger do, such that you lost your freedom in the present moment? You see, anger somehow was able to take away your self-control. Why was anger able to take away self-control? That's the next question. What do you think happens?"

Finding Awareness

He thought for a few minutes. Then he said, "*I feel stuck. I don't know, I guess.*"

"*Don't give up so easily. This takes work, so if we get stuck on the path that we think is the correct approach, and so far our approach feels correct to me, then it means we must put the same question differently. Let's reframe the question. Can you think of an example, when your partner said something, and you lost self-control as a result of it?*"

He immediately spoke, "*Yes, just yesterday she said that I care more about my friends than I care about her, and that made me very angry instantly. I lost control.*"

"*Let's slow down. We are trying to see why something would make us lose control over the present moment, right? What were you in control of during that conversation, and what changed the instant she said those words? To simplify, what did you lose control over in that incident?*"

"*Over myself?*"

"*Not quite. That's superficially true, but remember we are looking deeper, right? Within yourself what did you lose control of when she saw you as someone who doesn't care about her?*" I implored him, stressing on that last part.

His eyes lit up, "*Oh, I got it now. I lost control of how she thought about me.*"

"*Right, we discovered that we get angry when we can no longer control how someone thinks of us, how they see us. We want them to think of us in a certain way, and when they don't, we lose it. You want her to always believe that you care about her. When she doesn't agree with that narrative, you lose control over it. You lose control over the way she sees you.*"

"*That's making a lot of sense to me. And I can never get inside her mind and, I guess, change anything. I feel that intuitively and resent the loss of that control. Instead, I get angry. But why do I get angry? What has anger got to do with she not seeing me the way I want her to?*"

He was beginning to get the idea. I let him proceed.

The Art of Observing

"Good question. What do you think anger has to do with it?"

"So, if I get angry only when I lose control, it must mean that my anger is a way for me to wrestle that control back from her?"

"Right, anger is a way to get back what you lost," I said.

"I see what you are saying. I lost control, then I got angry to gain that control back. I lashed out at her because I lost control. Wait, that doesn't make any sense!"

"Or, does it make absolutely perfect sense?" I asked.

There was silence between the two of us. I could see him processing these thoughts in his mind. He had discovered something on his own. He had stepped into his own power.

"Wow, that blows my mind. I get angry at her, but the cause for it is me? Which means I can no longer blame her for my anger. I am angry not because of anything she says, but because of the simple fact that it makes me lose control over something within me. That's so true! Sometimes I don't lose my temper, and when I look back, those are also the instances when I felt in control of the situation."

"This means what then?"

"It means that I am not really angry at someone else, but at myself for losing control?"

"Isn't that interesting? How have we spent our whole lives blaming others for making us angry, whereas it has always been us? If we could always remain calm, then we would never lose control, and there would be no reason to get angry."

"But what about the fact that it's not true. I can't be calm because what she accuses me of isn't true. I do care about her, and yet she keeps saying those things?"

"Are you angry because it's false? Examine it. Let's say it is true, that you don't care about her, hypothetically speaking. Then at best you would be sad

141

for her having said the truth, right? Also if what she says is false, then you would most certainly ignore it, for what is there to be upset about, if it's not true? You see, the factuality of the statement, whether it's true or false, is not connected to anger at all."

"But what if there was an element of truth in what she said?"

"Right, an element of truth would mean that you don't know for sure whether it's true or not, right?"

"This comes back again to me. It is because I lack clarity that I get angry. Nothing to do with her."

"Correct."

"So then how do I find that clarity? How do I know for sure whether I love her or not? Because unless I do, I can't be calm when she says so."

"Right."

"So how do I find that clarity?"

"That's a separate matter which one has to go over in depth in a different meditation. That meditation would be 'Let me see if I love my wife' and you will have to make time, sit and go into it yourself, just like we are doing now."

"I see. So all of this means that the anger always comes from me. There is no other cause for it."

He was quiet for a minute, then he spoke again.

"But I have another question. What if I am too concerned with the way she sees me? What if, regardless of the truth, whether I love her or not, I want her to always feel as if she is loved? I want her to see me as someone who loves her."

"That depends on what you value more, love, or the perception of love?"

"I see what you mean. As long as I act responsibly, and show her love and care for her, what does it matter what she thinks or believes, right? If I do my job right, she will see it, and if she doesn't then I am either not doing what I am supposed to, or perhaps it's something else on her side of things. Either way, I would have done my best."

"That's all we can do. Do our best."

"If I did love her, I would not be not controlling her perception about me. Love is not controlling her right? That would be a form of violence towards her. I would never want to do such a thing. That's not me."

"Now, you see? This is insight."

He seemed moved by what he had come upon. A deep contradiction was brought to light and instantly dissolved.

"As they say, let go of what you love and it will come back to you if it's real. I never understood its true meaning, until now."

This is how we ended that conversation.

~

This is *insight meditation*. Going deeper into a question until an insight presents itself. The understanding of a question itself is the answer. That is why we never look for answers during insight meditation, we look for ways to understand the question better. In the process we see the question in a new way. *That new way is the answer we were looking for.* This is an exploration, and as such it is different each time. Yet, if we can practice this meditation diligently, a method begins to emerge. If you want to study this in more detail and understand what specific questions to ask and when, please refer to the Q&A section on insight meditation.

When insight meditation takes off, it becomes a tool that sharpens the mind. With experience, it can sink into the subconscious, such that when we face a challenge in daily life, an insight appears shortly thereafter on its own. If it doesn't, then the mind makes note of its inability to solve the problem. Then we can take the problem into a meditation and go deeper until an answer reveals itself. When an insight is found it

Finding Awareness

creates space in the mind. We feel clear and energized. Insight meditation is a skill. The way we get better at it, like any other skill, is through practice. As we have more insights, our mind begins to free itself from its burdens. We feel a renewed sense of self-trust and confidence, for we are able to resolve our own problems without leaning on someone else. The more insights we have on our path, the more sure we can be that we are headed in the right way. That way leads towards inward clarity and personal power.

NOTE:

Insight meditation is the answer to the second question we raised at the end of Chapter 12 - *How do you resolve past unresolved experiences?* The above conversations are the answer. They show us how the past can be reinterpreted and resolved. The resolution of our inner conflicts releases the mental energy trapped by those thoughts. Old experiences complete themselves as our past begins to make more sense to us. We begin to feel as if our suffering is finally coming to an end.

Once insight meditation deepens we start watching our daily life as it unfolds. We realize that our inner monologues are full of labels, judgments, and conclusions. We realize we have firm beliefs and strong attachments. Soon our insights begin to knock on the deepest doors of existence and begin to unravel the structure of our ego itself.

From here our path narrows. We have to be more careful and specific as we wade deeper into our own minds. The first thing we encounter are our myriad judgments about all things big and small.

Part 3

Structure of the Ego

20
Labels and Judgments

Judging helps us pretend that we understand.

What is a label? When we pick out something to purchase in a store, we know what it is by looking at the label on the product. When we have a cold, we go to the cabinet and look for the right medicine that will help us feel better. We want to make sure we don't accidentally take the wrong medicine. We carefully read what the label says. Without it, there would be no reliable way to distinguish one object from another. As such, labels are useful and necessary for everyday existence. They help us organize our world. From our science to religion, everything in human society requires labels. Without them, it's hard to distinguish, identify and, therefore, manipulate our reality in any meaningful way.

Though, why do we use labels in our inner world? It appears we do so for the same reason – to differentiate our emotions and feelings. For instance, how would we know what kind of an emotion we were feeling, if we couldn't use a word to identify it? If the word *fear* didn't exist, we wouldn't communicate to our loved ones that a certain thing was concerning us. If they had no labels of their own, they wouldn't know what we meant unless they had a common definition of the word *fear* too.

Finding Awareness

In this way, labels are essential. They allow us to define our outer and inner world. The more accurate they are, the better they describe natural phenomena. For instance, we have hundreds of dog breeds in the world. Unless we could differentiate between them, we wouldn't know which breed makes a good shepherd and which one a retriever. Labels in that way are neutral in nature. What happens when they have a meaning or a quality associated with them? Then they become what we refer to as *judgments*. For instance, you can say, "*This is a pitbull*" and that is just a label. However, if you believe, "*Pitbulls are dangerous,*" then that's a judgment.

A label is like a noun and a judgment is like an adjective. Judgments (or adjectives) too play an important role in describing our world. For example, take the case of our hunter-gatherer ancestors. How could they tell each other whether certain parts of the forest were dangerous or safe? Or whether some animals were docile or dangerous? Whether some flowers or snakes were beautiful, yet poisonous? How could they describe other tribes as friends or enemies, as kind or cruel? Whether they used verbal cues or physical gestures, they had to describe their environment in some way.

Judging also helped them make split-second decisions, which often would be the difference between life and death. It was better to misjudge danger than to misjudge safety. It was better to err on the side of caution. This has been going on for millenia, and there is no reason for it to stop now. That's why we judge everything even today. Judgments – such as good, bad, beautiful, ugly, dangerous, safe, kind, friendly, hostile, or cruel – are indispensable to human communication. Without them, we would struggle to get through a simple sentence. Therefore, the act of judging isn't wrong or right, *it just is.*

Yet, the most common advice we get is to be less judgmental. How do we reconcile this with the fact that we judge a restaurant based on the quality of its food, a movie based on the awards it won, the quality of someone's art based on their popularity, or a book based on its reviews?

Labels and Judgments

Most of us advocate a religion, a political party, a philosophy, or a spiritual teacher over the other. We prefer one musician, actor, athlete or a sports team over the other. All our life choices have implicit judgments behind them. This contradiction has a good reason.

Judgments offer an immediate comfort in a world full of uncertainties. Judging helps us pretend that we understand. Once we say, "*That person is cruel*," it gives us a feeling of certainty and completion. Our job is done. Now we feel as if we can predict the future and that gives us security. We don't have to do any work the next time we interact with them, since we have already put them in a bucket and formed an image about them. Even if this image is wrong, it makes our life easier for the moment. Therefore, throwing caution to the wind, we judge.

Does this mean that there are no cruel or evil people in the world? Perhaps some of us prefer to use softer words, such as unconscious, misguided or brainwashed. Yet, regardless of the words we use, we are still judging them, aren't we? And we must. It is obvious that if we don't judge those who are indeed cruel, to be cruel, then we are allowing their malice to spread in the world. One look at the wars of the past century makes it clear that calling out destructive forces in the world is essential in order to stop them from becoming powerful. So then, we have reached a point of conflict.

How can we identify cruel or unconscious behaviors while making sure we aren't judging people unfairly in the process? So how do we solve this problem? Should we judge or should we not?

Perhaps, a better way to look at this is asking whether the judgment itself is *correct* or *incorrect*, and more importantly, whether it is *temporary* or *permanent*. Let's look at both of these. Evaluating our judgments, instead of the act of judging, helps us to resolve this internal conflict.

Correct judgments deepen our understanding of the world, and reduce our collective suffering, while incorrect judgments do the opposite.

Finding Awareness

An incorrect judgment brings us into conflict with *our* reality. When we incorrectly judge another human being for being rude, stupid, intelligent or kind we take misguided actions based on that understanding. We avoid the right people from our lives and gravitate towards the wrong ones. We seek superficial experiences and avoid the ones that lead to growth and learning. We take up a job that is wrong for us, invest in a poor business idea, or enter an unhealthy relationship, all because of incorrect judgments. Correct judgments bring us into alignment with *our* reality, and therefore help us make the right choices. They may be difficult in the short term but in the long run they reduce our suffering, because they are fundamentally correct based on a given situation.

This is why the correctness of a judgment is not based on our (or someone else's) opinion, but on our experience and observation of how it aligns with our own personal life and its challenges.

A correct judgment happens spontaneously when we learn to put all mental chatter aside and simply look, feel and observe our life situation. The more deeply we observe, the more precise our judgments and decisions become and the more peace and clarity they bring to our lives.

Why do our judgments, both about ourselves and others, also need to be temporary?

Understanding something is like climbing a never-ending ladder. Every correct judgment is the next step on such a ladder. If we stop at a step, believing that it is the end, we have formed a conclusion. If we become comfortable and stop here, we become blind to any new information about the things we have judged. We get stuck with our beliefs, dogmas and limitations. This place becomes a reason for conflict, because the world and the people around us are always in flux. Our understanding of them soon becomes obsolete, stale and incorrect. If we don't change and adapt, we harbor rigid and outdated views about people and our life. Such a fixed outlook breeds contempt and fear of those we have judged.

Having temporary judgments allows us to constantly absorb new information coming from others. This way we can understand people in real time, never forming any permanent opinion of them. We have already seen how to do this through the arts of *listening* and *seeing*. These skills assist us in dissolving our current judgments and enter a state of constant watching and learning. They keep us moving on that ladder and flowing with the present moment. When we *hear* and *see* with intensity, we begin to notice hidden aspects of people's personalities and behavior. We spot the occasional kindness in someone we thought of as cruel. We notice sparks of brilliance in those we thought of as dull. We perceive hints of selflessness in the midst of all the self-seeking. We begin to understand their past and how it may be playing a role in their actions. We inch closer to knowing who they are as human beings.

We develop a more holistic understanding of the people in our lives. Sometimes we realize that those who deeply hurt us were hurting too. Now, instead of condemning their actions we begin to ponder the reasons behind them. Our anger begins to transmute into compassion and it invites us towards forgiveness. We will see more about how this happens in the next chapter.

So as we intensify our capacity to listen to and observe others, our judgments become increasingly *accurate* and *temporary* in nature. We become more open-minded, curious and forgiving. We begin to see people and the world not as fixed points on a canvas, but as a part of a large and colorful painting that is evolving, transforming and reshaping itself.

NOTE:

As we saw in this chapter, a judgment stands in for real understanding and brings short-term comfort. Why does it do so? Why does a judgment have this power to make us feel that it must be true? For instance, no one ever believes that their judgments are false, do they? They feel as if their evaluations are capturing the *truth* of the matter, especially our judgments about ourselves. To understand this, we have to find out where our judgments come from. We are entering the depths of our ego.

21
Beliefs

Our confidence in our judgments comes from the staunchness of our beliefs.

Since I started writing on Instagram in 2018, I have spoken to thousands of people both in person and over the web. Sometimes our conversations would span days or weeks, as we would continue exchanging ideas and thoughts about a certain issue. For about a year and a half, I conducted these discussions without sharing any personal information about myself.

One particular follower had been reading my work for more than a year and had asked me several questions over this period. Some of them related to her second divorce and her son, who was almost my age. Our discussions would sometimes continue over many days via Instagram messaging. All this while, she never asked my name, how I looked, or even what my gender was. We never exchanged any personally identifiable information whatsoever. She seemed content with how our talks were going, I was happy to be anonymous and so was she.

Eventually, as time went on, I began to get multiple requests from other readers to share a picture of me along with more details of my personal life. It seemed like I had gone on long enough without telling anyone who I was. For me, it was always about the message. However, I obliged because it felt right; the time had come. So I uploaded a picture of me with my dog.

The next morning, as I opened my message inbox, it was filled with responses from various people, most of whom seemed surprised. The first message was from her. *"All this time have I been talking to you? I am so embarrassed. I spoke to you believing that you were a woman in her sixties. This is the end of our conversation. Thank you."* Needless to say, I never heard from her again. Some of the other messages I received were, *"You don't look anything like I pictured you"*; *"I didn't know you were a man. Men never understand my problems"*; *"I thought you were a woman, though you sound much older than you look"*; and so on.

In their defense, I probably should have told them who I was sooner, although I wondered why the messenger mattered as much as the message. They had formed a mental picture about me, *based on certain beliefs*, and they expected my appearance to align with that mental image. Every time we hold a belief we begin to form judgments based on them.

In the previous chapter, we saw what judgments are, in this chapter let's see where they come from. There seem to be three different sources, the third of which, our beliefs, is most relevant to our inquiry into the ego. However, let's briefly look at the first two sources first before we dive into our beliefs.

The first source is our natural makeup. Some of us, for instance, may like to eat our food heated, while some of us prefer cold salads. Some of us prefer bright colors in our homes, while others like pastel shades. Some of us love to go on outdoor adventures, while others prefer to curl up in bed with a good book and a blanket. Some of us love to visit old cities with ancient architecture, while others prefer spending time in national parks and forest wilderness. Some of us think dogs are the perfect companions, while others can't live without cats, and so on.

Beliefs

These are our preferences – our likes and dislikes. However, they often manifest as judgments. For instance, you might hear someone say, *"Cats are mean. I love dogs"* or *"I don't understand what's so wonderful about cities. I prefer spending time in the woods."* Even though these claims sound like judgments, in reality, they are just preferences. When someone states their preference in the form of a judgment, it may create a minor conflict, yet fundamentally, preferences tend to be harmless. They rarely introduce any real problems in society for there is nothing objectively right or wrong about them. Yet, they are important to note, so that we can better isolate true judgments from mere preferences in our relationships. If it's a preference, then there is nothing to be done about it. It doesn't need to be correct or temporary.

The second source of our judgments is our cognitive biases. For instance, if we meet someone from a particular country, who is warm and kind to us, we form a judgment that all nationals of that country, on average, are kind and polite. If we meet someone new who resembles us in appearance, we tend to trust them more compared to a person who looks different. Or when we read advice about meditation we assume those who have given it must have been around for a while, and so on. There are more than one hundred types of these biases identified in scientific literature. As interesting as they are, we won't be covering them. Even though out of our scope, they have to be identified as a significant source of incorrect judgments in our lives.

This brings us to the third source of our judgments – our beliefs. Judgments arising out of beliefs are the root cause of inward and outward conflict in the world. *Our confidence in our judgments comes from the staunchness of our beliefs.* The stronger the belief, the more deeply we are convinced that our judgment must be true. The weaker the belief, the more flexible we tend to be with our assessments. If we prefer, as we saw in the previous chapter, to have judgments which are both correct and temporary, then the beliefs from which they stem ought to be loosely held. *Entrenched beliefs can't lead to flexible judgments.* Let's look at some examples of social and personal beliefs to further clarify this.

Social beliefs

Our social beliefs mainly consist of our religious and political ideals. For instance, those of us who have been taught to believe that our religion holds all the answers, naturally judge other religions as misguided. Let's be sure that we are simply examining how beliefs work, without criticizing or justifying them. Those of us who happen to deeply believe in the idea of a god are also likely to judge someone who is an atheist to be immoral. Religious beliefs happen to be the most common source of moral judgments. This seems to be true for politics too. The stronger our belief in our political ideology, the more harshly we judge our fellow citizens who believe the opposite. We judge our fellow humans based on their *beliefs*, and not their actions. While expecting others to judge us based on our actions, and not our beliefs. On many occasions I have seen people holding the opposite beliefs as me, commit acts of kindness and generosity far surpassing what I have been capable of. Yet, I found myself judging them based on their beliefs, and not what I just saw them do. I invite you to observe these contradictions in your life, and invoke them when you question your beliefs.

Unfortunately, the judgments our social and religious beliefs produce tend to be unforgiving in nature, for they are closely related to our identity (which we will look at in a later chapter).

Personal beliefs

Perhaps, what we believe about ourselves plays the most important role in the way we choose to live our lives. A positive set of beliefs generally leads to a more open and confident approach to living, while the opposite leads to more fear and hesitation. However, what we believe about ourselves, as with anything else, lies on a spectrum. One end of it is a positively narcissistic belief that whatever we want, we automatically deserve. On the other end lies a belief that we are destined to suffer, that we don't deserve to be loved, find happiness or be successful. Somewhere in the middle one could perhaps find balance.

> The core set of beliefs that we grow up with are usually formed in our childhood.

If our parents provided consistent and reliable upbringing in our early formative years, we developed positive and beneficial core beliefs. Our core belief system is built upon self-assurance and resilience. On the other hand, if we were brought up by emotionally unavailable or inconsistent parents, the opposite beliefs – that we don't deserve happiness or love – takes root in our minds. In this case, our core belief system is built upon doubt and fear. These core beliefs in most cases weren't taught to us, we simply assimilated them by witnessing the way our parents were living their lives.

If as children we saw our parents being overly self-critical, grappling with addictions or always feeling unhappy, that helped form our definitions of how life is to be lived. For instance, if we witnessed our parents get divorced through a long, painful process, we begin to believe that marriages were not meant to last. As adults, some of us become more likely to push away those who bring happiness and stability to our life, for it reminds us of the pain a possible separation might bring. We can't let it happen again, no matter what the cost. We become emotionally cold and unavailable, especially if a commitment is required of us. What can we possibly do? We deeply believe that commitments are a gateway to pain and loss.

A similar thing happens if, as children, we were neglected or abandoned by our caretakers in some way. It forms a belief such as *"I don't deserve to be loved,"* for what else could explain their departure? The core belief then is built upon guilt and self-blame. When we grow up with this belief, every time we have a relationship issue, we judge ourselves to be the

Finding Awareness

cause of it. We think, "*He is going to leave me just like my father did when I was little, and it's all my fault.*" In my 1:1 sessions, I have spoken to several people who experienced some form of abandonment as children. Most of them felt the same fear of abandonment in their current relationships. What's more is that they strongly felt they deserved it.

Challenging our beliefs

It seems that all these beliefs, both social and personal rely on one thing – our inability to question them. We have gone on to live our lives without ever seriously asking ourselves whether our beliefs are, in fact, true. This deliberate challenging of our beliefs is fundamental to dislodging them from our psyche. Let's look at how this is done.

The way to challenge a belief begins by remembering how it was formed over a period of time through certain experiences. If we can identify the core memories [10] and incidents that created the belief, we begin to see how most of our beliefs are tied to a certain time and phase of our lives.

That those beliefs apply to an old version of us,
which no longer exists.

That they were perhaps limited and contextual, never meaning to be applied to the whole of our lives. For instance, if someone said, "*You are not good at swimming,*" it applied only to that one sport when we were ten years old, nothing else. It has no bearing upon us now. Come to think of it, we didn't care enough about swimming anyway, yet that remark took root and held us back in other areas of life.

Here are some examples on how to challenge our negative self-beliefs. Each one of these may take days to slowly work through.

---
10   If a core memory can't be remembered, it perhaps doesn't exist. It's not advisable to undertake hypnosis or other methods to remember supposedly repressed memories. The human brain has been shown to create imaginary memories if it is pressured to remember. If something did happen, it will come to you clearly, without any effort or doubt about its existence. It's better to forget than to misremember.

For instance, "***Is it really true*** that I was not good enough as a child or is it just a belief I have learned to live with? Did my parents say those hurtful things only because they had a standard set by my older brother? What if I was the older brother? What if I was the only child they had? Then, could they have compared me with anyone? So, their judgment about me seems to be based on arbitrary comparisons. Everything I have accomplished so far in my life stands on its own. It proves that I am capable of succeeding irrespective of what anyone else may think. This is a false belief and I can let it go now."

It's clear that such questioning of one's beliefs takes the form of insight meditation. As we have seen before, insight meditation requires a firm inward connection to our sensations. We have to feel centered in our body through practicing undivided listening, seeing and feeling. Therefore these examples do not work, unless there is that inner feeling of safety through which we are looking at our beliefs. If we aren't centered, we can't feel safe. If we can't feel safe, we can't let go. In other words, *we can't let go of a belief if we feel unsafe without it.*

So as you read these examples, take a deep breath and find your rhythm of breathing. Listen to the sounds around you intently, feel the sensations moving across your body, and scan your room with your eyes. When you feel centered, proceed.

Let's look at some more examples.

- "***Is it really true*** that I don't deserve to be loved, or is this just a belief I have stopped questioning? My father left us when I was little. I remember that day. What would have happened if someone else was in my place and I was able to watch my own family as an impartial observer? Would my father still have left his only child and it's mother? Perhaps, yes. That means his behavior had nothing to do with me. I don't have to blame myself anymore for his actions. I am worthy of being loved. Indeed, I have people in my life who deeply love me. I deserve to be loved."

- "***Is it really true*** that I am to blame for what happened, or is this just a belief I am unable to let go of? I remember clearly that I was repeatedly abused as a child. I remember how it all unfolded and I couldn't refuse. But I was only a child. How could I have known any different? A child has no role to play in what happens to her. Therefore, I was not responsible for what happened to me. I can't go on blaming myself for someone else's actions. I can forgive myself and let go of all this guilt. I can live my life now for the past has no bearing upon my present."

These four words, *"Is this really true?"* have great power in them. They have been my guiding light. When we question our firmly held personal beliefs, it becomes possible to forgive ourselves. This forgiveness reinterprets and resolves our pain. Sometimes even years of hurt and fear is released in a matter of minutes and we realize that we are kind, trustworthy, compassionate, intelligent, and worthy of love. We remember that there is nothing inherently wrong with us at all, only with our beliefs.

At any given time, we all have a mixture of positive and negative beliefs driving our judgments and life decisions. Whether they are self-critical or self-exalting, we act as if all our beliefs reflect reality. When we question and disprove our beliefs we feel free and empowered. However, if someone else, or life events do it for us, we feel threatened and insecure. It's best to challenge our beliefs before someone else does, for then we know our truth before someone else exposes it. For instance, if we question our belief that we are a gifted artist and discover it to be false, it causes us no real pain. However, if our peers in the field disclose this bitter truth to us, it brings a profound sadness. We become confused, agitated and violent. Why does being wrong in our beliefs create so much confusion and fear, especially when someone else proves us wrong? Why do we have this insistence on being right with our beliefs? Why does being wrong cause suffering?

Beliefs

It does so because we are attached to our beliefs, and where there is attachment, there is always suffering.

> NOTE:
>
> Let's summarize what we have discovered so far in this section. As we centered ourselves and began our journey inwards, we first encountered our judgments. When we looked closer we discovered that our judgments arise from our beliefs. Then we questioned our beliefs to interpret and dissolve them. In doing so it appears that our beliefs are powerful, because we are attached to them. The path shows itself again, as it invites us to look at our attachments.
>
> As we descend into the depths of our ego, our journey is becoming harder. We are required to examine more, search deeper for the answers we seek. For some of us this part of the journey feels confusing, and we are eager to abandon it midway. However, this process of intensification is a necessary step. It is preparing us for what lies ahead. Let's see how much further we can go and what else we discover about ourselves.

22
Attachments

Attachment is a process by which we seek security *from others*, but only find *insecurity and suffering* in return.

My grandfather raised a family of six in a tiny house in the suburbs of Mumbai on a mere pittance of a salary. He was strict and demanding of his four children. Everyone had to sleep at the right time and wake up early. Everything had to be clean, tidy, and, most of all, in its right place. If a piece of candy cost more than half a penny, it was too expensive. If you broke your shoes, you had to wait your turn to get a new pair. If you wanted new pants, you had to wait until you grew out of these ones. He was a disciplinarian. Right up until he passed away a few years ago at the age of 84, he would clean the entire house by himself. It would take him three hours, but he would do it all the same.

All of his children, including my mother, suffered the brunt of his unyielding nature as they grew up. He was very kind, but only when you least expected him to be. Sometimes he was curt or indifferent, also when you least expected him to be. He had a short temper, but he loved me. I spent a lot of time with him when I was growing up. I might even have been his favorite grandchild, or so I thought, until one day, I went too far.

Finding Awareness

I used to go to my grandfather's place right after school, since it was close by, and wait for my mother to finish work and come pick me up. One of the things I used to find amusing about my grandfather was his reading glasses. Describing these glasses is quite a task, for they didn't look like glasses at all, but a distant memory of what once were spectacles. They were at least 25 years old then. The only thing that had changed within those frames were the lenses, as they grew increasingly thicker with time. The temples opened so wide that when he put the glasses on, I would wonder how they hung onto his ears at all. The six-year-old me was always fascinated with this relic and wanted to put them on.

One day, when he was not in the house, I snuck them out of his cabinet and carefully put them on. I looked around the room and tried to balance them on my head. Then I wanted to see if I could look at my own hands. Needless to say, the moment I looked down, they dropped on the floor and shattered. When my mother came to pick me up in the evening she wondered why I was sulking in the corner. One look at my grandfather's face and she knew something had happened. He didn't have his glasses on and his face was strained, as he tried to repair his broken pair with a tiny screwdriver and some glue. When I told her what had happened she began to laugh. She walked me over to a small closet and opened a different cabinet.

Inside it were three new pairs of glasses, barely used. They were all my grandfather's. I asked her why was he so angry with me when he already has three new pairs? She smiled and said, "That's the first pair of glasses he ever bought, with whatever little money he had. You see, he's deeply attached to them."

What are attachments?[11] We only say two things are attached when they were originally separate. We never say our arm is attached to our body,

---

11 The word attachment is used in a different sense from its use in the 'Theory of Attachment,' which is part of psychology. It's best to clearly state as such to avoid the confusion between the two. The 'Theory of Attachments' has various types of attach-

because it's a part of our body. Therefore, implied in that word is a suggestion that perhaps whatever we are attached to is not a part of who we are. It's something we have taken up in order to feel a connection, a bond, or security.

This security can come from material possessions, money, social status or from our ideas, opinions, and beliefs about the world. Sometimes this security comes from other people. In every case, the object of our attachment becomes a source of comfort and safety for us. A reverse way of putting it is whatever provides us emotional security is at a risk of becoming our attachment.

For example, let's say we buy a new house and spend a lot of time painting and decorating it. Then we give house tours to friends and family who compliment us on how spacious and beautiful it is. They notice how there's plenty of light entering from all directions, and our keen eye for aesthetics and say how wonderful it is in every way, and so on. This praise satisfies a deep craving for acknowledgement within us. The house now becomes a source of validation and acceptance. It makes us feel deeply secure for a moment. When our mind clings to that security, an attachment is born.

Now, what happens when someone doesn't like our house or our friend moves into a bigger house than ours? Suddenly the source of security we feel is cut off. We feel anxious, jealous or angry. This is suffering. The deeper our attachment is, the more suffering it causes. This happens because attachments rely on a spurious and temporary connection to security. When the uncertainty inherent in life breaks this connection (as we saw in Chapter Three), we find suffering. This is what my grandfather felt when I dropped his pair of glasses. When they broke, so did his connection to the false security that they gave him. Attachments, in this way, are always to an *external* source of security and what is external is

---
ments, the way this word is used in this book, it has no types. Perhaps a more accurate way of describing it would be a 'hang-up', as described by the British philosopher Alan Watts.

by definition beyond our control. Anyone could damage our car, or say something about our house, or prove us wrong in a debate. As such, we have no way to prevent the pain they can give us.

> We chose that pain when we got attached.

This is easily seen when we are attached to physical objects, but gets harder as those objects become more subtle. As we look at our inner lives, two kinds of attachments seem to be most common. The first is to our beliefs and the second, to other people. This is why at the end of the previous chapter we discovered that when anything we believe in turns out to be false, we feel pain, for we were attached to those beliefs. Our beliefs gave us security.

Before we proceed, let's address a common misconception first – that the opposite of attachment is detachment. It's natural to think so because of the way language works, yet that can be deceiving. We saw this in the chapter on fear as well. The opposite of fear was not courage; it was fearlessness. Similarly, the opposite of attachment is not detachment, but freedom. A forced practice of detachment may lead us into another conflict, for without understanding attachment, we are bound to misconstrue the word detachment. We may practice aloofness or carelessness in our relationships believing that we are free from attachments. That is clearly not the case. Such a practice may hurt our relationships even more. Therefore, let's examine our attachments and see what they reveal.

Attachment to opinions and beliefs

If we are attached to our opinions and beliefs, we rely on them being accepted by others. For instance, let's say we give someone advice that they asked for, and then they reject it, how does it make us feel? When we recommend a movie or a song to a friend and they dislike it, what happens? When we have an idea at work and our colleagues reject it, how do we respond? We feel as if they don't value us. We feel hurt and insecure.

It feels as if we aren't seen or loved. Their rejection broke our access to security that those attachments gave us.

So our attachments became a source of validation from others. These attachments are the only way we can satisfy our deepest cravings for human connection and security. This relates to what we saw in the chapter on insecurity too. That for the most part, we know ourselves through outside validation, not through our own. However, through our journey since then, we have tried to understand ourselves on our own terms, without relying on any approvals whatsoever. We have studied our insecurity, loneliness, fears, pleasures, guilt, and suffering in detail. We centered in our bodies and doubted our deepest beliefs. This cumulative increase in self-awareness and self-knowledge gradually illuminates the dark corners of our mind. It moves us towards *becoming the source of our own security*.

Now, even if the world thinks we are mistaken, we can think for ourselves before accepting their version of reality. If the world thinks we are wonderful, we don't accept their empty compliments either. We listen without accepting or denying. In the process, we free ourselves from the attachment to our opinions and beliefs. If there is no attachment to being right, being wrong no longer causes suffering.

> This is the freedom from others' opinions and our own, for the only source of security we rely upon is our independent and free self-inquiry.

Attachment to people

This brings us to a deeper form of attachment – that to other people. We even confuse it with love. Attachment only feels like love, but it isn't. Love has no expectations, while attachments are filled with expectations. Love asks, *"What will make them happy?"* Attachment asks, *"What will make me happy?"* Attachment manifests in ways that make us feel as if we care for others, when in reality, we only care about how their behavior

Finding Awareness

affects us. A mother pressuring her daughter to marry may think that her concern comes out of love. Yet, when she examines her own mind, she discovers that her daughter's defiance has become a topic of unpleasant conversations in the family. That a fear of what *others will say* plays a larger role in her desire to see her daughter married, than her professed love for her child. A controlling mother may thus discover that her self-image and reputation take precedence over a genuine concern for her child's happiness.

An emergent theme in my talks with my readers was their strained relationship with their mothers. The love in their relationship was contaminated with attachment. Love requires freedom in order to breathe. Attachment, on the other hand, requires control to survive. A controlling parent passes down all their fears, insecurities, and self-limiting beliefs on to their children. We saw how this happens already in the chapters on fear and beliefs. Under the pretext of protecting their child, the parents are protecting themselves. In the process they teach their children to fear life the same way and hold the same flawed beliefs that they do.

A parent who loves their child goes to great lengths to prevent these attachments from being formed. No matter how uncomfortable it feels, they protect their child's freedom of thought and build their child's self-inquiry. A loving parent passes down their strengths to their child, while filtering out their weaknesses. They understand that attachment and fear go together. They are easily formed in the child if they are careless. Love and freedom also go together, but they are difficult and require a lot of care and attention. Therefore to raise a child free of attachments, a parent has to first understand and shed their own attachments, for children learn more through observing their parents actions, than listening to their words. Right parenting arises naturally from right living.

Intimate attachments

When it comes to our intimate relationships, attachments create expectations from our partners. When these expectations aren't met,

Attachments

our language and behavior changes. It becomes verbally and psychologically violent. If we are forceful, our partners feel threatened and create emotional barriers to protect themselves. We explored this in the chapter on violence. Attachments, in that sense, accomplish the opposite of what they intend to. Instead of bringing two people together, it pushes them apart. Instead of bringing down divisions, it creates barriers.

Now, there are certain basic expectations we have from our partners which don't come from our attachments. They are intimacy, trust, communication, and a feeling of physical safety with them. How do we know these are not attachments? Because they did not arise as a result of us seeking any emotional or physical security from our partner. They existed even before we entered the relationship. They did not develop over time, as a result of us leaning on our partner for emotional strength or validation. They were always there as basic building blocks for any association. *This is why, expecting our partner to help around the house, or take care of our child is not an attachment.* It's simply a part of them fulfilling their basic responsibilities. Calmly communicating about these expectations to a loving partner can prevent them from escalating into a crisis.

However, if we expect our partner to solve all our emotional problems or rely on them to *take care* of us when we are facing a challenge in our lives, that's an attachment. Attachments, if we carefully watch them, are a pulling force. They seek towards the center, the ego. They are all about '*what I want*'. That is why they have the opposite effect. They push our partner away. If we are attached to our partner, we are also deeply in conflict with them. Attached relationships tend to be full of tension and pain. Each person is relying on the other to address their own insecurity and fears. It soon becomes a transactional relationship.

Attachment says, "*You provide me with emotional, physical or sexual security and in exchange, I will put up with your abusive behaviors that nobody else will.*" Such a relationship depends on these two-sided attachments to function. They fulfill each other's insecurities with false securities, and enable each other's dependence. Such a relationship knows no freedom; only a subtle form of leverage and control. They are entangled with each other. Possessiveness, jealousy, emotional meltdowns, perpetual discontent, and helplessness are common in such a relationship. They are trapped to such a degree that even the idea of freedom makes them insecure. The solution then isn't to practice detachment, but to become aware of our attachments as we act them out. The strong correlation between seeking security *from others*, and repeatedly finding *insecurity and suffering* in return is the key to letting go of our attachments. As we saw earlier, when our self-knowledge grows, our fear and insecurity begins to dissolve. We realize that *true and lasting* security comes only from within, *not* from someone else.

This happens when our relationship with ourselves becomes meaningful and we begin to feel secure in our own company. As we become the only source of our emotional strength, our attachments naturally begin to wither away. They leave behind freedom and space. Even if one person takes up this responsibility the other gets pulled into this process, for they find no reactive tension in their relationship. They feel freedom, love and acceptance emanating from the person who is becoming self-empowered. Now, the love which was being smothered by attachments, begins to breathe, and spread its wings.

NOTE:

We saw in this section how our judgments arise from our beliefs. Then we saw how our beliefs gain their power from our attachments. Then we looked at how attachments become stronger when we seek external security through objects, ideas or people. However, why does the thought of being free of attachments create an existential threat in some of us? Why do some of us feel that if we aren't attached, we can't be in a healthy loving relationship? We feel as if we may become aloof, detached and unable to connect with anyone. This deep fear is triggered because of yet another part of our ego, our ego-identity. We seek *ourselves* through our attachments, therefore the thought of losing them brings up a feeling of losing ourselves. This is also why when a relationship ends we feel utterly lost. We don't know who we are without our partners. We face an identity crisis for months or years that follow. This is the same fear my grandfather felt when his glasses broke too. He saw them as a representation of his life's struggles. He didn't want to lose them, for they reminded him of who he was.

23
The Three Selves

Say to yourself, "Don't give me your story. Give me your truth!"

At the end of the previous chapter we saw that we seek ourselves through our attachments. That *self* is what we are concerned with. Who is this self we are seeking all the time? The answer to this came out during a video conversation I had with one of my readers during my fourth session with him. We had spoken about many different subjects and were nearing the end of our talk, at which point he asked me this question.

"I have a question about the ego. I find it quite hard to understand. I don't know where to begin. Can you give me some pointers about how to learn about the ego?"

I thought over it for a few seconds. Then I asked him, *"How many egos do you think are a part of this conversation?"*

"What do you mean? You and me of course. Two egos, unless there is someone else listening to this," he said, with a little concern.

I said, *"Yes, there is."*

"Okay. Who is listening?"

Finding Awareness

"We have had six egos listening to every conversation we have had. Three of these were on your side and three on my side."

"That doesn't make any sense. But it seems like there is more to it."

"You see, we are not one person at all, but three. At the center of our ego isn't one self, but three different and overlapping selves. Therefore even if we think of ourselves as individuals, we're not. Our ego is splintered from within."

"I find that unbelievable and quite strange. What are those three selves?"

"First, who you think you are (your self-image), second, who you show the world you are (your self-projection), and third, who you actually are (your true-self). These are the three selves."

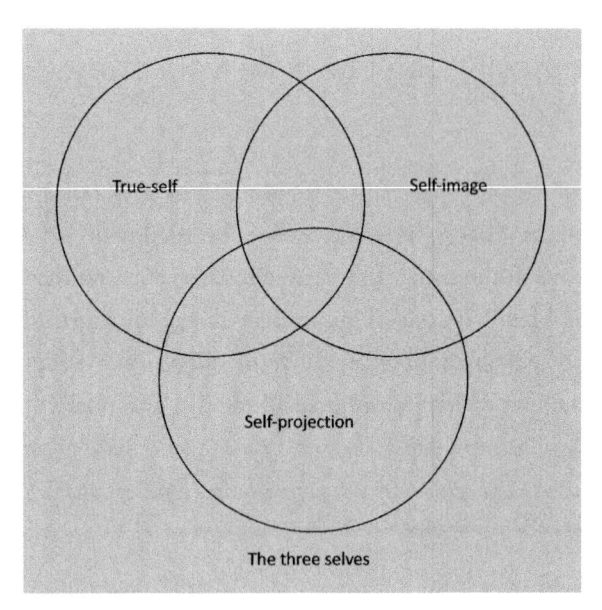

The three selves

"So when we discussed attachments a little while ago, you mentioned that we seek ourselves through our attachments. Which of these selves is the one we are seeking?"

"The self-image. For that's the only self we think we have. We are mostly blind to the other two."

"Would you mind discussing these three selves in a little more depth? I feel like they are related to the ego in some way."

"They are. They sit at the center of the ego structure."

The rest of the chapter, and the next, is a summary of our conversation, as we discussed the three selves and the divisions they create. We may be urged to conclude that since we are talking about our ego-self, a singular, there must be only one self we have. Yet, it is quite clear that it can't be the case. For when we tell others who we are, we sometimes confuse it with who we *believe* we are and, moreover, who we *should be* for the sake of the world. It seems as though our self is broken down into three parts, and each of these are important to understand. They point to the fundamental inward division and disconnect we feel within. Let's start with our self-projection.

Self-projection

Most of us have a specific role or roles we play in society. For example, if we have a job, we have to fulfill the responsibilities that come with it. In order to do so, we have to dress a certain way, speak in a professional manner, manage our delicate work relationships, and occasionally self-advocate for a promotion. This is our work role.

In our personal life, we have other roles to play. If we practice any art form like painting, then we play the role of an artist. If we are passionate about yoga, mindfulness or music, we want others to think, *"She's an artist,"* or *"She's a yogi,"* *"She's a healer,"* or *"He's a musician."* In addition, we are also mothers, fathers, daughters, etc., in which case we play even more roles as caring parents or children.

These roles construe an image about us that we want people to hold in their minds. We try our best to shape this image as positively as we can. This is our self-projection, which includes our reputation and social status. The simplest way to identify it is to ask ourselves, *"How do I want others to see me?"* If we can imagine seeing ourselves through the eyes of our family, close friends, coworkers, that's our self-projection. It's a combination of these roles along with the qualities associated with them, such as a *generous* friend, a *loving* mother, a *gracious* host, a *wise* teacher etc., is all our self-projection. It is our ticket into society. We use it as a means to gain acceptability in the world.

Behind this self-projection, there is another self, which is who we *think* we are. For example, "*I am a great artist,*" "*I am a good writer,*" "*I am an advanced yogi,*" "*I am a good mother,*" "*I am physically fit,*" or "*I have a great sense of humor.*" This is our self-image. Notice the words, '*I am*' that identify our self-image, compared to the words, '*she is*' or '*he is*', that identify our self-projection. Our self-image is a picture of ourselves, in our own eyes, as opposed to self-projection, which is how we should appear in others'.

The self-projection tends to be an embellished version of our self-image. That is, we tend to overestimate our abilities and virtues, because doing so increases the probability of social acceptance. This social acceptance is security. It's a valuable currency. It makes it all worth it. For instance, if I was a photographer, the picture I would show everyone would be the one out of a hundred others that didn't come out so well. If I am a yogi, the pose I showcase is the one I have mastered. If I am applying for a job, I amplify my accomplishments in my application. Most of us are guilty of this subtle deception because it helps us.

Our self-projection is an idealized version of our self-image. It carefully avoids our (perceived) flaws, failures, and vulnerabilities, unless displaying them is somehow beneficial. For instance, when we see that appearing vulnerable can make us look more authentic, then we act vulnerable. It now becomes a part of our self-projection. Then we could even exaggerate our flaws in order to look more genuine. Our self-projection serves a simple purpose – to get us some favor and acceptance in society. Whether it's through self-deprecation or self-promotion, tends to be of little importance.

Self-image

By contrast, our self-image serves no such purpose. It is purely a function of what we think, believe, and feel about ourselves. For instance, if we are overly focused on our past failures, regrets or apparent shortcomings, then we tend to have a negative self-image. If we are focused on our achievements, goals and how fortunate we are, then we have a positive self-image. This goes back to the chapter on beliefs, where we saw how our positive and negative personal beliefs shape our decisions.

> All those personal beliefs come together to form our self-image. It is how we perceive ourselves to be.

True-self

When we question both our positive and negative personal beliefs (as we saw with examples in the chapter on beliefs), we begin to go deeper into our psyche and discover our true-self. In doing so we discover which of our beliefs are false and which are true. Our true-self emerges as the *factual reality* of who we are, beneath the layers and layers of suppositions and speculations. This part of our self remains hidden until we say to ourselves, *"Don't give me your story. Give me your truth!"* When we are no longer satisfied with the protective shell of our self-image, our true-self begins to shine through.

This fragmentation between the three selves is the reason why we are so inwardly conflicted.

To summarize:

- True-self + beliefs (positive, negative, correct, incorrect) = Self-image
- Self-image + idealization = Self-projection

Finding Awareness

Though it seems as if they should be concentric circles, with self-image being inclusive of the true-self, and the self-projections, being inclusive of our self-image, that is not the case because of the incorrect beliefs that we hold about ourselves. If we have to represent the three selves visually this is how they would look. The intersections of their boundaries creates some distinct phenomena we routinely experience in our lives.

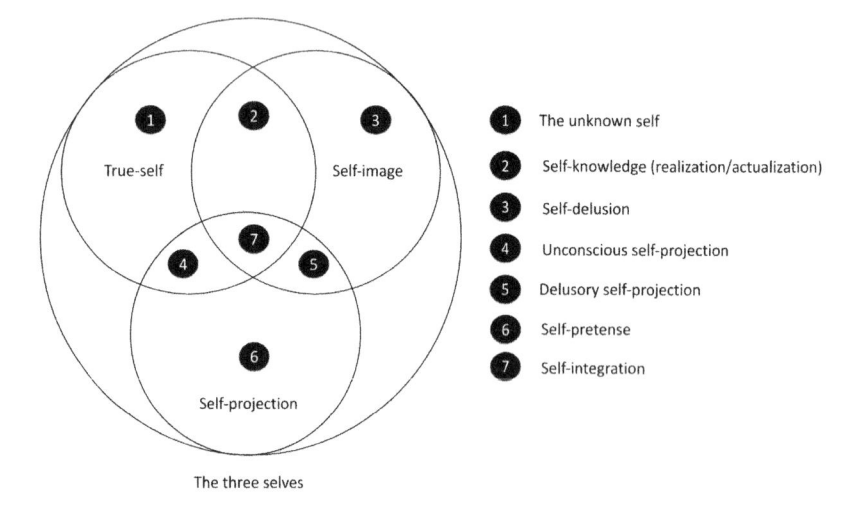

1. The unknown self
2. Self-knowledge (realization/actualization)
3. Self-delusion
4. Unconscious self-projection
5. Delusory self-projection
6. Self-pretense
7. Self-integration

The three selves

1. *The unknown self:* Parts of me I am still unaware of. For example, fears and desires that have not yet come into my conscious awareness.

2. *Self-knowledge:* Things I know about myself through self-awareness.

3. *Self-delusion:* Things I believe I am, but in reality, *I am not.* However, I don't showcase these to others. I keep them to myself. For instance, a belief such as, *"I don't deserve love."*

4. *Unconscious self-projection:* Things others can read about me which I am not aware of, but are true of me. For example, the various biases and prejudices that I may hold which I unknowingly display in my actions. I don't think I believe

those things, but my friends *know* I do. For instance, a belief such as, *"Men are smarter than women."*

5. *Delusory self-projection*: I *think* I am these things, and project out to the world. Though the reality is these qualities don't exist within me. For instance, I think I am the smartest person in the room, and act like I am, though the reality may be opposite.

6. *Self-pretense*: I pretend to be someone *I know* I am not. For example, I willfully lie and mislead people for my own gain by convincing them that I have their best interest at heart. For instance, I betray the trust of my partner by lying to them.

7. *Self-integration*: Things I know about myself to be true, and those are precisely the things the world sees. For instance, I know I love animals, because I work many hours rescuing and providing for them, and the world knows this to be true as well.

Self-integration is the part of ourselves where we actually are who we think we are, and it's the same person others perceive us to be. Could these selves ever merge into one? Could our ego ever become whole, integrated, and free its divisions? If the three selves could merge into one, we would become individuals *in the truest sense of that word.*

NOTE:

Before we see how these three selves can be merged, let's see what we have witnessed so far. We started this section with judgments. We then traced their origin to our beliefs. Then we studied our beliefs and realized that they get their strength from our attachments to them. Then we examined our attachments. Our attachments, when disturbed, cause us pain. When we looked for the source of that pain, it led us to the ego-identity or the self. When we investigated it, it appeared that the ego-identity was divided into three. Now, let's examine if the self can be healed from this internal divide it suffers from and find the integration that it needs.

24
The One Self

"Why did I exhaust myself trying to be someone else's version of me, when being myself was so effortless?"

As we saw in the previous chapter, our true self is who we are in reality. It slowly merges with our self-projection and self-image as we observe our behaviors and thought patterns behind them. It is worth noting that we are using the words *true-self* in a different sense than its ordinary usage, which is a higher-self or an aspect of universal consciousness. In the context of this book, the true-self is simply who we are in all our messiness and glory. It is not magnificent in any way. It is an ordinary fact, not a supposition. When we consider our true-self to be something grandiose, we imagine various qualities that ought to go with it. Such inventions only delay self-integration, because they condition us to reject anything ordinary. They fuel the inner conflict, for reality is usually quite simple.

So how do the true-self and the self-image come together ? What does that process look like?

Merging our true-self and self-image

As our self-awareness deepens, we become more aware of this true-self. For instance, let's say we thought of ourselves (which is our self-image) as someone who is full of humility and decided to examine this closely. As we observe and question this humility, we see a different side of us emerge. We remember instances of how we pretended to be humble, when the situation called for it, but not otherwise. We could stage being humble when there was a benefit associated with appearing to be so. We notice how our humility sometimes had undertones of egotism and pride to it too. For example, when we were criticized, instead of humbly listening, we lost our temper and blamed others. If we were ever denied credit for our work, we asserted ourselves and demanded the praise we deserved. Our self-image says, "*I am humble,*" but our true self shows us that beneath that veneer of humility, there are often shades of vanity. It reveals that perhaps we are not as humble as we thought. This is an expansion of our self-knowledge.

The moment this realization happens, a little bit of our true-self merges with our self-image. The conflict between *who I am*, and *who I should be* subsides. This conflict rages on only as long as we are blind to our actual behaviors. When we notice what we are doing unknowingly, the conflict disappears. There is no more, *"I should try to be humble"*. There is only, *"I am however I am"*. The *becoming* turns into *being*.

Sometimes these insights are of the opposite nature. That is, if our self-image contains a limiting belief that we are not deserving in some way. Upon questioning, that belief corrects itself.

I once spoke to a reader who was dealing with self-esteem issues. Her parents pressured her throughout her childhood to be at the top of her class. They wanted her to be a doctor. She managed to live up to their expectations for a few years, but at one point, she failed in a class. Her self-image crumbled under the weight of their pressures. The last few years had been an uphill battle trying to please her parents. She felt depressed yet could not talk to her family about it, for they were the ones who caused it.

When we questioned her self-image together, by looking at the facts of her life, it became clear that she was drawn towards the subtlety and expressiveness of music. Deep down she wanted to be a singer. That was her calling. (Chapter 26 goes deeper into discovering one's calling). She was a trained classical vocalist and had recorded and written several songs. Here she felt no limits, no shame, no fear, no pressure. So I asked her why she wouldn't pursue something that she loved? She said because of uncertainty and the possibility of failure. Then she realized that she was fighting failure and uncertainty even to *chase a goal her true-self did not care about*. The moment she had this insight, she saw what she was caught up in. The fight to become what her parents wanted her to be was over. Her self-image and true-self had met each other. Their conflict had come to an end.

Still one question remained, what of her self-projection?

Merging our self-image and self-projection

As we saw in the previous chapter, our self-projection is an idealization of our self-image. If that self-image itself is based on something we don't truly want to be (such as a doctor), then how do we face society? How do those two parts of the self come together?

When I spoke to that same reader a few months later, she said, *"When I first told my family that I am no longer going to push myself to get into the best medical college, they were really angry. They felt betrayed. I told them I am still planning to become a doctor, but I won't struggle simply because they want me to. I am doing this for me, not for them. I will do it at my own speed without any pressure. If I change my mind tomorrow and drop out, so be it. It will be my decision. I know who I am, and I am going to build on my strengths and not grapple with what they think are my weaknesses. I feel so free now. I sometimes wonder, why did I exhaust myself trying to be someone else's version of me, when being myself was so effortless? I want to sing, and that's where my heart will always be. That's who I will be to the world."*

She had a sudden fearlessness about facing everyone. As her self-image corrected itself, her self-projection did too. Where did this sudden change come from?

Our self-projection hinges on one thing – *our fear of not being accepted*. It is this fear that makes us focus on our weaknesses and forget our natural strengths. It forces us to look for faults within us and patch them up before anyone else finds out. It doesn't want us to appear vulnerable. This is why it becomes exhausting to play a role for someone else. On the other hand, it takes no effort to be oneself, because we already are ourselves. We can't do this because most of the time we don't know who we really are. When she discovered who she was, it became exhausting for her to keep up with the pretense of being someone else. It wasn't worth it anymore.

Ego integration

With the shedding of our false beliefs, and the end of all pretenses, the borders of the three selves begin to dissolve, and a single self emerges. This is the integrated ego. The 'I' in the center *now* feels like a single person. A cohesive whole begins to form at the very core of our being. A deep turbulence within ourselves comes to an end. There is effort saved and energy released. Everything within us feels connected, because we know who we are. Our thoughts become sharp and clear. When we know, we know. When we don't, we don't. There is no hesitation in between. There is only the peace that comes from self-knowing.

NOTE:

As we have seen in this chapter, ego-integration depends on self-awareness. The more self-observation and awareness we practice the more this process of integration continues within us. The reader I spoke to had discovered what gave meaning to her life. That fundamental insight made her fearless and brought about the integration of her ego. We are all in the middle of this inquiry, waiting for the purpose and the meaning of our lives to be revealed. This is an important question that we will discuss in Chapter 26.

However, we have now come to a point where the entire structure of the ego is about to reveal itself for we have studied each of its components (judgments, beliefs, attachments, ego-identity) in detail. In the next chapter, we will draw this structure so that we understand it, but first, I want to tell you how I came upon it.

25
Structure of the Ego and the Feeling of Me

You, me, and everyone we have ever known, at the very center, are nothing but this *me thought,* each with their own unique history. In that sense, we are all unique, and yet the same.

This was an incident from a time when the old structures had just begun to crack, and a new way of being was taking over. The specifics of it don't matter to me and putting this in print seems absurd, but it serves the path which we find ourselves on. This was a time when some deep attachments had broken and I found myself in the middle of suffering and pain. The past was painful, and the future, uncertain. There was only one place I wanted to be and that was the present moment. I was practicing the centering meditations of breathing, listening, feeling and seeing, all the time.

This was more than a decade ago when one of my close friends was getting married. One of my other friends and I were going around Mumbai, my home city, looking for a set of personalized luxury fountain pens. After hours of searching we were directed to a boutique shop tucked

Finding Awareness

away in a corner of the expensive section of the mall. It was a hot summer day and we welcomed the thought of being indoors for a while.

As we walked towards the store, the mind was intensely present. The eyes were scanning every inch of space they could see. They noticed the depth, the shapes, and the texture of each object that they came across. They saw all the faces that passed us by, never fixating on or judging them. The ears were listening to the tiniest sounds they could hear, catching bits and pieces of passing conversations as the words arose and disappeared into the deep silence from whence they came. The skin could feel the rustling of clothes against the body. In the middle of all that noise and clamor, one could perceive a faint rhythm, the heart beating against the chest. There wasn't a single thought being processed in the mind, there was only presence.

The showroom was brightly lit and had various items arranged neatly in rows behind glass cabinets. Two store employees, a young man and a woman, approached us, dressed in plain, unassuming clothes. They asked us what we were looking for and we began to strike up a conversation. As this was happening, an intense form of listening had taken over. Every word had a cushion of silence around it. Amidst all of that was happening, the mind was focused on the one who spoke and the sound of their voice. There was nothing else. As we continued talking, it became apparent that they understood very little about the nibs, inks or the engraving process itself. They had recently taken up the job to pay off their college fees. The man seemed like he came from especially scarce means and was eager to do well in his new job. Making this sale was important to him. He was hesitant and genuine when he spoke, even though he said little.

A particular innocence was betrayed by his mannerisms and his voice. He had a strange simplicity so rare among human beings that once it is noticed, it becomes impossible to ignore. An intense presence began to build up as the mind noticed this strange and uniquely beautiful person. The innocence and utter lack of deceit began to expand and overflow from his being. It seemed as if it would soon fill up the whole room.

As I listened to him speak, I had a strange feeling that I was slipping away into a state of bliss. I stepped out of its way; it came forward and took me. Then it happened.

As he spoke, I felt as if it was not he, but I who was speaking. A state of existence in which I couldn't sense myself anymore. It was me who was behind the counter, speaking to this person and his friend trying to make a purchase. I couldn't be sure if the vision was real. It felt as if the mind had dissolved its own boundaries and became unable to discern where the self ended, and the other began. For those few minutes, all its problems were gone. There were no desires, no fears, no goals, no ambitions, no suffering, no pain. There was only that state of rapture, for the center had ceased to exist. I had never experienced a true connection with another human being before. But when it happened, a total stranger became me. In those few moments, all his problems were mine. All his sorrows were mine. Even though I hadn't the faintest idea what those were. All I knew was that I would have died for that man if that's what the moment called for, because he was me. The mind had somehow stepped beyond its limits and discovered true compassion. It might have even discovered love.

~

For the next few years, I had no idea what had happened that day. I don't believe in analyzing these experiences and, as such, I was no closer to understanding them. However, once during insight meditation a question arose, *"What is the boundary of the ego? Where does one person end and another person begin?"* A memory of that experience came back and began to unravel its mysteries. As I thought more about it, I remembered how in order to escape my suffering; I had decided to be fully centered that day. I was practicing listening, seeing and feeling at all times. When I felt that surge of compassion for this stranger, the boundary of the ego

Finding Awareness

suddenly dissolved. Its structure collapsed and the feeling of separateness disappeared.

The *state of total awareness* somehow was able to end all inward divisions. Yet, it wasn't a permanent change. When the wholeness of that state splintered, it broke into thousands of familiar fragments. All the internal divisions returned. That division, between one ego and another, was revived once the experience ended. Not only that, but all my problems were back too within a few minutes. My fears, desires, attachments, beliefs, and memories had returned, and so had my existential battle with them. I could feel the conflict between fear and courage, confusion and clarity, sorrow and happiness once again. As I remembered and observed that experience, two questions arose.

Why had all my problems disappeared in the first place, and why had all of them suddenly returned?

These questions seemed too intricate at the time, as perhaps they seem to you now. They also appeared too conceptual and irrelevant to the daily ups and downs of my life. Which is why I left them alone for years. Yet, once they unraveled, it brought profound changes in the way I treated myself and other people. This is what I discovered.

The structure of the ego

So, why had all my problems disappeared? They disappeared because for a few minutes there was no *'me'*, trying to control *'my fears'*, or a *'me'* trying to solve *'my problems'*. There was no inward division anymore (It's okay to not fully understand this division at the moment. We will explore it in more detail later in this chapter). *I* was at peace with *myself*. When this happened, the structure of the ego temporarily collapsed. There was, for those few moments, the ability to feel real compassion for someone else.

If so, why did the problems suddenly come back? Why did they not stay gone?

Structure of the Ego and the Feeling of Me

They came back because the conflict between the ego and its myriad belongings resumed, and the ego resurrected itself. This happens when there is a strong desire to change what is unfolding. If we see a fear come up, and we want to address it, right away the old conflict is reborn as the 'I' tries to do something about *'my fear'*. With the rebirth of this conflict, comes the regeneration of the ego, the divisive factor of our inner experience. However, as the ego resurrected itself, it also revealed its secrets. Its structure was now clear. This is how I believe it looks.

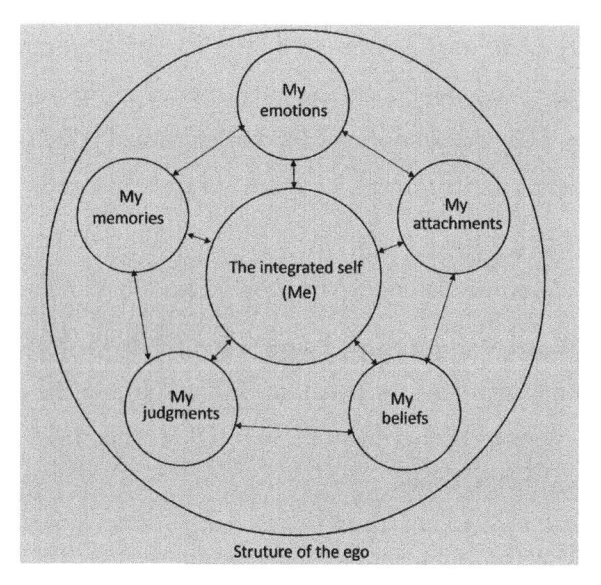

Struture of the ego

The outermost circle shows the boundary of each individual ego. The innermost circle is the integrated-self or the ego-identity which we saw in the earlier chapter. The rest of the circles are the ego's belongings. Just because our ego-identity is integrated doesn't mean that all our inner conflicts are over. It only means that there is no conflict between who we are, who we see ourselves as, and who we show the world. There is still the division between *'me'* and various mental objects, such as *'my attachments'*, *'my memories'*, *'my beliefs'* and *'my judgments'*. This division is so common and ubiquitous that asking someone to see it is like asking fish to see water. Let's understand this division, for it is the *greatest source of confusion in all of self-understanding*.

The ego and its belongings

The best way to understand this division is by studying our relationship with physical objects (outside our body) and how it is similar in nature to our relationship with mental objects, such as our emotions, which are inside us.

Take any object, like a tree outside your window. If you can observe that tree, it means you are separate from it. It also means you can go towards it, climb it, water it, or cut it down. When you are separate from an object you are observing, you can interact with it. This subject-object distinction is fairly simple when we are dealing with physical objects. You are the *observer,* and that tree, your phone, or that chair is the thing that can be *observed.*

What about mental objects, like beliefs, emotions and memories?

We have seen in our journey how when we decide to, we are able to examine our emotions, such as fear. We can observe the fear within us, just like we can observe that tree. So it follows that this fear must be something separate from us.

> Come to think of it, why else would fear seem like an emotion that is outside of our control?

We are constantly fighting our fears, aren't we? If it were a tree, it would be our intention to cut it down and burn it. So, all the evidence we have indicates that fear, like an object, is separate from us, because we can act upon it in some way, yet it's also within us. The same principle applies to all our emotions, judgments, attachments, beliefs, or memories. These are mental objects apart from the self, yet contained within the ego boundary. This is why the structure of the ego looks the way it does. This is why we feel divided from within.

Now, it also becomes clear that all of the ego's belongings are nothing but thoughts. The integrated self – which contains who we think we are, who we project to the world, and who we actually are – is also made up of thoughts. The whole content of our ego is nothing but thoughts interacting with each other with one thought taking center stage, the *feeling of me*.

The feeling of me

This *feeling of me* is a powerful thought that seems to have assumed superiority over others within the ego. It arises from that circle in the center, the integrated (or still in the process of integrating) self. It encompasses and includes all of what's in that circle. That is why when we say the word 'I', we speak from all three aspects of our identities simultaneously: who I am, who I think I am, and who I show the world. Everything is included in that center thought, the *feeling of me*, or the '*I-thought*'

It is a thought that has access to all our experiences, memories and emotions and is willing and able to manipulate them. This is the thought that is living our life right now. You, me, and everyone we have ever known, at the very center, are nothing but this *me thought,* each with their own unique history. In that sense, we are all unique yet the same. That's why we all have this peculiar physical sensation in the chest. Even though a thought is in our brain, we point to the center of our chest when we refer to ourselves. This association between that *tenseness in the body* and the organizing thought together manifests as the *feeling of me*. It is both our unique and shared reality.

This *feeling of me* wants to maintain order over our fears, hurts and desires from running amok. It wants to maintain peace and harmony in its internal environment. It stems from the ego's desire to bring about change in itself. How we go about this change matters immensely, for it decides whether we further this inner conflict, and strengthen the ego, or rise above it. This brings us to the next turn in our journey – understanding how change happens within us.

NOTE:

It may appear that ending the ego is our final goal. It isn't. For the ego, as we have seen on this path is *our teacher, not our enemy*. It is by watching this teacher that we learn. Whether the ego occasionally leaves or stays is of absolutely no concern to us. It is not a special event reserved for the few (which is another ego story), but a thing that happens to all of us multiple times in an ordinary day. When we look at a sunset, play with our dog, or hold our children and forget about the worries of the world, our ego is gone. All those instances are times when the ego momentarily disappears, for it has nothing left to teach us. It is when we return to our old ways of resistance does the ego come back to educate us in the form of suffering. As always, our path calls us to examine the process of inner change our ego tries to bring about in itself. This feeling of me, which is at the center of each of our egos, tries to transform itself. Let's see the different ways in which change enters our life.

Part 4

The Struggle

26
Presence and Planning

When your passion meets your responsibility,
it becomes your purpose.

He said, *"I have read probably a hundred self-help books and I think I understand myself pretty well. Yet, there is one question that I have never been able to resolve."*

"Well, let's look at it. What is your question?"

"Let me lay some groundwork first. When I first got into self-help, it was through reading books on positive psychology. They helped me immensely. They inspired me. I wanted to change myself and they seemed to have all the answers. But they all spoke about bringing about outward change. That is, they spoke about becoming successful in life. Making more money, attracting whatever you wanted, etc. After reading them I would feel motivated for a few days. I would make up some goal and chase after it. Soon, I wouldn't be able to sustain it and return to my original and familiar state of confusion. I would go from feeling inspired to depressed, and back to inspired. This happened over and over again. Though after I went through a rough breakup, everything changed. Suddenly, I began finding spiritual books very comforting, as opposed to positive psychology. Instead of inspiring me to chase goals, they

turned me inwards. In short, I have enjoyed following both approaches, the outer as well as the inner."

"Yes, this has been my experience too," I said.

"However, these days, I have gotten deeply into spirituality, and I am mostly happy where I am."

"Mostly?"

"Yes, mostly, because when I look at some of my friends, they are setting these lofty goals and working hard towards them. One of them has his own business, while another one is trying to get into a top medical school. When I compare myself to them, I wonder if I am making a mistake with all this 'navel-gazing', as my brother calls it. He is an aspiring novelist."

"So what is your question?"

"I think I am seeking inward change. On the other hand, they are seeking outward change. I wanted to know which kind of change I should be seeking? Have I become addicted to this inward looking? Am I lost? When I seek only outward change using positive mindset training, I feel empty. Then when life happens and suffering comes, those methods stop working. I turn inwards. Yet, when I seek this inner road, it is often very quiet and lonely. It doesn't lead to direct changes in my life. The grass seems greener on that side."

"So is your question about knowing which is right? Planning, which your friends are doing, and presence, which you are seeking? Are you trying to figure out the difference between the path of inward change as opposed to the path of outward change, and how they relate to each other?"

"Yes. That is it. I am confused about how to structure my life – around inner change or outer change, around presence or planning. I am confused about whether I should just pick an outward goal and chase it, or should I go deeper into myself and wait for the answers to come. How deep am I supposed to go in order to bring about change in myself? It's all very frustrating. The speed of my life is so much slower than theirs."

"This is a great question. When our ego tries to uplift itself, it looks at these outward achievements as the primary way of seeking change. It looks at the way society defines success and begins to chase after popularity, impact, wealth and all those things which are good indicators, perhaps, of outward success."

"This is what I believe too. That they are all expanding their egos through their ambition. They are seeking fame and popularity, so I ignore them and just put my head down. Then I feel like I am judging them, while being short-sighted. I can't tell what's real and what's not. I keep going in these circles. It's so confusing."

"Let's take a step back, okay? Not all those who are doing ambitious things are seeking to expand their egos, right? We have to be careful in approaching this, because it is very easy for the ego to cling to some self-comforting delusion then have a rude awakening ten years later."

"Right, so how would you approach it?" He asked.

"Broadly speaking, there are two approaches to change. Inward and outward. Let's first discuss the latter and see where it leads us."

"Yes. I am quite interested in putting this confusion behind me so I can feel confident in what I am doing with my life."

"Seeking an outward change in life is to set a particular measurable goal and pursue it, right? Whether it's starting a business, or getting into medical school or whatever it may be. So, when do you think we can have a certain goal? Where does it all begin?"

"With knowing what you want for yourself?"

"That's right. If you don't know what you want, you can't aim for it. If I give you a map, and ask you to find your destination, you'll want to know two things. What are those things?"

He thought for a few seconds then spoke.

"Where I am, and where I want to go?"

"Correct. So even if there was a map in life (which there isn't) with a clear set of instructions, you can't use it unless you know where you are, which is self-knowledge, and where you want to go, which is also a product of self-knowledge. Do you see it?"

He nodded. *"Yes indeed."*

"That means without clarity about what you want, the question of goal-setting or planning does not even arise. We look at others achieving their goals and we wish the same for ourselves. It's natural. Yet, only a few of us ever see what's hiding in plain sight – their remarkable clarity about who they are, and what they want, and why they want it. Without this lucidity about one's goals, chasing them leads nowhere. If we simply pick up a random goal, without feeling strongly about it, we only get more confused. We may learn a few things from the experience, but fundamentally, we are still lost. Does this make sense?"

"Yes. It does. This is what I went through for many years. I would set goals which I did not fully believe in. They would just be fleeting desires and I would get sucked into them. Please keep going."

"Our demand for clarity is the first step. Whether we want to become a writer, or a painter, or a businessman is unknowable until we first find that clarity. Sometimes people refer to this as finding your purpose or calling. Some of us find this purpose early in life, some a little later. Some of us know precisely what it is, yet others know only the direction in which it lies. Some of us find it quickly and some have to wander a little bit. Do you get the idea?"

"So, are you saying my friends and my brother know their purpose already? They don't even practice any meditation. My brother is younger than me!"

"I am saying it's possible. We don't know, and we shouldn't care that much, to be honest. What we need to care about is whether we have that

clarity ourselves, and that's the only thing that matters, right? Besides, purpose is not a lifelong thing, or doesn't have to be anything glorious either. It can be temporary, and it can be humble. The only quality it has to have, is that it's true to you. You can feel it in your bones and your blood. It's real and alive, you understand? It becomes undeniable once you see it."

"So you mean it's flexible and also firm?"

"In my opinion, yes. All this will become clear as we dive deeper into how to find it. That is the next question which is arising from our inquiry: how to find that clarity, purpose or calling. Do you want to look at this?"

"Yes. As I said, I can't wait to put this confusion behind me."

"One thing is certain. Our purpose can't be something we don't want. For instance, I can't want to be an artist, if I don't like doing art. Would you agree? My purpose can't be, let's say, to be a good mother, if I don't love kids, right?"

"Yes. I see that. I agree."

"So that's where we have to begin. We have to find the things we naturally enjoy doing. I call these things drifts. You have to find your drifts, for they are already pointing you in the right direction."

"I have heard you say this before in your writings. What would you say to those people who don't enjoy anything? I personally do have a lot of hobbies, but I wonder what this means to people who don't have any."

"I don't believe it to be true. We all enjoy doing things. We are just not conscious about what we enjoy as we blindly stumble through our lives. When we examine our life a little closer, they show up. Perhaps we like talking to our friends, helping them with their problems, or watching films, or reading books. It can be anything."

"I see. So are you saying look deeper and explore a little to find out what you like, for the purpose can't be something you dislike."

"Correct."

Finding Awareness

"Okay, let's continue. You were mentioning drifts. I like that word. Drifts, though it makes it sound as if I am not doing anything, but going with the flow."

"That's exactly right. Your natural genetic makeup, upbringing, and experiences make you an individual who has certain likes and dislikes. You didn't choose them. They are there. You discover them when you stumble upon them, or feel a subconscious pull in their direction. I call them drifts because, when our mind is still, it gravitates towards those things."

"So what do I do with my drifts?"

"First, find them. What are the things that you enjoy? You said you had many hobbies?"

"Yes. I enjoy photography, playing my guitar, writing, and watching movies. I also love keeping myself fit."

"So photography, writing, music, movies and fitness are your drifts. Now, we ask a series of questions to these drifts, and see which one of them lives up to the standard that our purpose demands, okay? In order to do that we need to separate your casual interests from the things that you love."

"I see. How do I do that? I feel like I love all these things."

"Ask yourself these two questions. One, which one of these things make me lose track of time? And second, which one of these do I have a natural ability in? These things tend to be the ones we really love doing."

"Hmm. I love watching movies. I do tend to forget time when I am engrossed in a film. But, I don't think I have any natural ability here. So movies can't be one of the things I love, right?"

"That's right. Keep going. What else do you see?"

"With photography too, I seem to have a natural skill, but I don't make that much time for it. I am just too lazy to go places and take pictures. So I am guessing this is out too."

"If you say so. What about music, fitness, and writing?"

"I think I love them. I seem to have a knack for these too, and I do get a little carried away sometimes. I have spent endless hours learning music, reading fitness blogs and developing my writing skills."

"So now we move on to the next stage. We ask which one of these are my passions?"

"So drifts, loves and passions. How do I find that out?"

"A passion has three specific qualities to it. First, we lose not just our sense of time, but also a sense of self while engaging in it. Which means we feel as if this is something greater than us. We are doing it for a deeper cause, something subtle and beautiful is present here. Next, we are willing to stand our ground for these things we are passionate about. We are willing to face opposition. If my family doesn't want me to be a musician, and yet I defy them, then music is my passion. Third, we lose sight of extrinsic rewards. We follow a passion with little concern for any external rewards or praise. So three conditions need to be fulfilled. Whatever survives these questions tends to be a passion."

"This is much deeper than I have ever examined my hobbies. If that's what a passion is, then fitness surely doesn't qualify. For even though I can go to the gym, in spite of what someone else might say, I don't look at it as something larger than me. I might even be doing it as a vanity project. Extrinsic reward is front and center. I want to look good, as much as feel good. So, I don't think it's a passion of mine."

"Okay, what about writing and music?"

"With writing and music, I do feel that these arts are quite subtle, and I often lose myself in them. I do feel I am devoting myself to them. There is some extrinsic reward in writing, but it doesn't seem like that's the main reason why I do it. I simply enjoy expressing myself. The reward is just an icing on the cake. I am beginning to see that, maybe, I am a lot more like my brother than I thought."

Finding Awareness

"Let's focus on you. Your brother has his own battles to fight."

"Right, right. Let's keep going. What do we do with our passions?"

"So we saw drifts, loves, and passions. Now we arrive at responsibilities. Usually the way we define responsibility is something which is a burden placed on us by society, but I mean it slightly differently here. The way I am using the word, it is to indicate a responsibility to yourself. You feel personally responsible to do something. If you refuse to do it, then you feel as if it won't be done properly. You also feel as if you have no choice in the matter. It's out of your hands. What's more, you have a unique vision about it, and want to do this thing a specific way, and that makes it personal. So three questions again. Do I have a unique vision about it? Do I feel personally responsible to do it? Do I sometimes feel like it is out of my hands and that I have no say in the matter? If you say yes to all three, then it qualifies as your responsibility."

"I deeply love music, and I am passionate about it, but I don't have any unique vision at all. I just try to play like those who I admire, and I'm satisfied with it. When it comes to writing though, it may be different. I am very intrigued by this approach, but I don't want to admit what you are confronting me with here. I feel I am not prepared to face this. I feel excited and yet deeply anxious."

"That's a good sign. You don't have to put it into words. Just know this, that when your passion meets your responsibility, it becomes your purpose."

He closed his eyes. It appeared that he had found an answer and was giving himself time to fathom it.

"I will need to process this in my own time. We started off by wanting to chase a goal, which is outward change, and we ended up inside the mind."

"Right. Now when our purpose is clear, we can begin planning. Rather, planning becomes possible only when we are clear about what we want."

"So this helps me see clearly what I need to do now. It resolves my conflict between presence and planning. They are not exclusive, but go together. They *can't exist without each other. But as I think about getting there, I feel uncertain. I feel afraid and anxious. I have this deep fear of failure and uncertainty within me, and it has only grown with time. In spite of reading so much about meditation and even practicing it, my fear has gotten worse. Do you think such a thing can happen, or am I losing my mind?"*

"No you are not. We may find our purpose, but getting there is a different story altogether. To get there, we have to first stop fighting ourselves. We have to get out of our own way."

27
The Backwards Law

The key to ending our self-sabotage lies in understanding when effort is the right approach, and when it backfires.

My fear of drowning began when I was seven. I was playing in the pool with my cousins, when I slipped and fell on my back. I spent about thirty seconds at the bottom of the pool, helplessly fighting to grasp onto whatever I could find. Fortunately, at the same time my father turned around and looked for me. Upon not seeing me where he expected me to be, he realized something had gone wrong. He rushed over and pulled me up. He turned me over at the side of the pool and water left my body as easily as it had gone in. However, it never left my mind. The trauma of drowning had made its home. I decided never to set foot in the pool again.

As I grew up, this fear began to recede. In my late twenties, I decided to take swimming lessons again. For the first few weeks, I remember struggling to get a handle even on the basics. There were many others like me learning how to swim and all of them made progress, except me. I just kept *drowning* no matter what I tried. The harder I tried to stay afloat, the faster I sank. After a few lessons of this thrashing about, the instructor

Finding Awareness

pulled me aside. *"Listen, just dive forward and lay flat on the surface of the water, okay?"* He said. *"The water will hold you. Just push off and let go."*

"No way I am doing that! I will plunge head first," I complained.

"Trust the water, if you want to swim," he replied. Something about the way he said it stuck. I decided to give it a try. I took a deep breath, stretched my arms high above my head, and plunged forward. As I did this, I glided along the surface for fifteen feet. I paddled and I kept going for a few more. I turned to one side, exhaled, and took another deep breath. I remember feeling ecstatic at what had just happened. I swam fifty feet without stopping. I felt relaxed for the first time in the water. I asked him why he had held this trick from me until now.

"Because you weren't ready for it," he said.

On my way home, I kept thinking about what had happened and what he had said. What did he mean by *I wasn't ready*? Was he implying that without that initial struggle, I wouldn't have trusted his advice? The more I thought about it, the more it seemed as if there was something else at play. It was my fear. It had me believe that I would drown if I didn't do everything in my power to stay alive. It had never let me relax since that incident as a child. It had primed me to struggle. I wasn't open to any other approach except to resist. I just couldn't let go.

When I ultimately did, I felt liberated. The water wasn't trying to drown me at all. It was my struggle that was making it happen. I wondered where else my past fears were forcing me to do the same? Where else was I drowning because I couldn't relax?

This pattern appeared in other areas of my life too. I was struggling in my career, in my relationships, and in my personal goals. I came to realize that this *trying, struggling, failing* and *trying* again, had become a habitual way of living. I couldn't notice it earlier because perhaps the trauma associated with them wasn't as severe. Yet incidents such as an embarrassment in school, or losing a pet as a child, or being bullied surely left behind elements of struggle which became cumulative over time. It caused resistance in daily life. It made me believe that if I was under stress, I must be doing something necessary and important.

If things felt difficult, life was normal.

There is another reason why we choose this struggle, in addition to fear. The second reason is simple: sometimes this struggle works. Sometimes, struggling, effort, force, and willpower take us towards our goal. We work hard for that job and we get it. We push ourselves to exercise and we lose that weight. We practice yoga and eventually become good at it. Believing this to always be the case, we apply effort everywhere and expect the same result. This is when our problems begin, for not all challenges respond well to effort. Some problems get worse with effort and we drown.

We can see hints of this when we ask someone to forgive us; when we try to move on from a relationship which has ended recently; when we try to relax when we are anxious; or when we fight our addictions with self-denial. We end up with this strange phenomenon where the *opposite* of what we expect ends up happening. The person we want forgiveness from moves further away from us. The more we try to forget who we loved, the more we remember them. The more we try to relax, the more anxious we feel. The more we fight our addictions, the more entrenched they become. This is the self-sabotage we spoke of at the end of the previous chapter. This self-sabotage is not done *on purpose;* it just *happens.* No one wants to be more afraid as they try to fight their fears, then why does it happen? It happens because they are unaware of the underlying principle at work.

Alan Watts, the author who introduced the western world to eastern teachings, called this principle the Law of Reverse Effort or the Backwards Law. It refers to instances where application of *mindless effort* has the *opposite* effect on the problem at hand. On the surface it seems fairly intuitive, yet how does it actually work? How can a mental pattern we

Finding Awareness

fight, take away our energy and become stronger in the process? Unless we understand this in depth, we are bound to unwittingly dig deeper into the traps we find ourselves in.

It happens because of this principle of *negation reinforcing* or, to put it simply, *what you resist persists*. First let us try to understand how this principle works, and perhaps in the process we discover when it applies and when it doesn't. For the key to ending our self-sabotage lies in understanding when effort is the wrong approach, and when is it necessary. Let's look at a desire, a pain and a fear and see how they respond when we use effort to fight them.

Negation reinforcing: Desire

Let's see how this process unfolds using two *opposing* thoughts. The first thought to consider is, "*I should get a glass of wine,*" while the subsequent one is, "*I should not get a glass of wine.*" Let's see how each of these thoughts are processed in two people. The first person who has these thoughts in that order is *addicted* to alcohol and the second person *isn't*.

Thought 1: "I should get a glass of wine."

The key word in this sentence is the word *wine*. In both people, this word triggers memories associated with it. We all know that when a memory is accessed we feel the emotions that are contained within it. We saw this in Chapter 12 too, when we studied the structure of our suffering. To recap, each memory is like a box that has emotions contained within it – some resolved and some unresolved. If the emotion is *resolved*, the box is closed and things are quiet. If the emotion is *unresolved*, then the box is open, and the emotion is active. This subconscious emotion has a charge, a momentum to it, because it is trying to resolve itself by creating spontaneous thoughts and musings in our conscious mind. This will become relevant later in the chapter.

Now, when this word *wine* is processed as a part of the first thought, emotional states associated with the memory of drinking are invoked in both these people. However, the feelings evoked in the addicted person are powerful, and those invoked in the other person are mild. Why? Because the person who has an alcohol addiction has a lot *more* unresolved emotion (as it relates to their drinking), compared to the person who doesn't. Their box is *open* and their emotional content is *active* due to their relationship with alcohol, which is laden with escapism, withdrawal, guilt, and powerlessness.

In other words, for a person who has an addiction, the mere mention of the word *wine* activates their addictive pattern, whereas in a non-addicted person it doesn't bring up any strong emotions whatsoever. Their box is closed and it remains that way. So now we have an addicted person whose desire burns with a powerful craving for alcohol and a non-addicted person, whose desire looks more like a calm preference for a drink.

Now, let's see what happens when both these people resist this first thought and apply *effort* to curb their desires.

Thought 2: "I should not get a glass of wine."

This thought captures the willpower we exert to improve ourselves. The more willpower we have, the stronger this thought tends to be. For the sake of this example, let's assume that both the people involved have the same amount of willpower, so their effort to negate or reverse the previous thought is about the same.

What happens when their minds reinterpret this word *wine* in their second thoughts? Both their minds have no choice but to invoke *all the associated emotional memory* to *the word once again*. In other words, when we resist a desire, we bring up the emotions associated with it *twice* – first when we have the original desire, and again when we resist it.

This means that the unresolved emotional content now arises with *even more* ferocity. We gave it something to latch on to in our conscious awareness. Remember, its original momentum is towards resolving itself

Finding Awareness

by creating spontaneous thoughts in our mind, and we just poured more energy into this process. We poured gasoline in the fire. This has a devastating effect in the mind of an addicted individual. Their original desire to drink now begins to rage. The more it intensifies, the more they resist and reinforce it. They get trapped in a vicious cycle that can only end in one way – with a drink.

We don't see this happen in the mind of a person who has no addiction to alcohol. When they say "*no*," their mind is able to change course and move on to something else. This reinforcement (from the second thought) isn't strong enough to make them drink because there was nothing significant in their emotional reserves to begin with. Nothing was rising up. There was no fire. Their mind was always *resolved* about alcohol, and it stays resolved.

Where else do we see this pattern of will-power and effort backfiring? This seems to happen with our painful and fearful thoughts too. The more we try to forget hurt, the more we remember it. The more we try to feign courage, the more afraid we feel. A pattern begins to emerge, for this aligns perfectly with the three unresolved emotions we studied in Chapter 12 – pain, pleasure, and fear.

In every case, when we have unresolved emotional content, using effort triggers the Backwards Law into effect. We bring about what we are trying desperately to prevent.

Let's verify if this is indeed the case with pain and fear too.

Negation reinforcing: Pain

Consider a painful breakup on the one hand, and the passing of our grandmother - of whom we only have fond memories – on the other. The breakup is an unresolved pain, which means we have intrusive thoughts about it. Our grandmother's memories are a resolved pain, for they don't intrude in our day to day life.

Now, let's say we catch ourselves thinking about our past relationship, then try to stop ourselves from doing so because it causes pain. What happens then? We only end up thinking more about them and the pain increases, right? But let's suppose we come across a picture of our grandmother in our family album and begin to think about her. After a few minutes we tell ourselves to move on with our day. Our mind easily drifts onto other things. So *unresolved* pain gets stronger, while *resolved* pain doesn't, when effort is applied. The process works almost exactly the way we saw with the desire above. The rising thoughts absorb our power and become stronger when we resist them.

What about fear?

Negation reinforcing: Fear

Fear, by definition, is unresolved. Fear is our resistance to past unresolved pain. If it is resolved, it is no longer fear but fearlessness. Like every unresolved pattern we've seen , it takes our energy and uses it against us. This is why the more we try not to be afraid of something, the more we fear it. Fear works exactly the same way as pleasure, with one key difference. Pleasure is a movement *towards* an experience and fear *away* from it. Take the two thoughts below and apply the same negation reinforcing process to them.

Thought 1: I am afraid that I will fail. Thought 2: Don't think about failure. The entire process that we saw with desire repeats itself. The more we try not to think about failing, the more we do. Thoughts about failure eventually bring about what they seek. We create a reality we were trying to avoid.

When does the law not apply?

What does all this tell us? There are certain conditions in which effort is the wrong approach. When we are fighting against unresolved portions of our own past, we are fighting against ourselves. There is no winning such a fight. For when we fight ourselves, even if we win,

Finding Awareness

we lose. Therefore the Law of Reverse Effort applies only in situations where *unresolved* emotions are involved. Our effort backfires. Our pain, fear or pleasure increases when we fight it. Wherever *resolved* emotions are involved, effort has the intended effect. Negation reinforcing doesn't happen. If we understand this principle, we get out of our way. We can stop tripping over ourselves and move fearlessly in the direction of our goals. *We can end the self-sabotage.*

However one question remains. What should be done in those situations where the Law applies? If effort is not the solution, what is? The possibilities raised by this question cause deep trepidation in us. They point towards the opposite of effort, which is *letting go*. We believe that if we take our hands off the steering wheel, even for a second, we will automatically head towards a cliff. The same way I believed that if I didn't struggle, I would have drowned.

Thoughts such as "*If I don't control my drinking, I will become an alcoholic*", or "*If I don't fight my fears and my pain they will overcome me*" begin to get louder. As you read this you may feel this fear too. This is a good sign, for it means we understand the gravity of our problem. We feel the immensity of what lies ahead. This brings us to the stage of our journey, where we face a difficult choice.

We are at a crossroads now. One path leads back to where we came from, towards the familiar methods of effort and struggle to solve every problem. The second is the unknown – the path where the old methods do not work. The known path, even if it gave us suffering, is still familiar, but this other path is dark and it stirs deep fears within us. This is the great unknown, a place which tests our resilience. Those who enter it will never be the same again.

Which path will we take from here?

Part 5

Surrender

28
The Precipice

When the dualistic forces within us feel as if our unstoppable will has reached an insurmountable obstacle, we have reached the precipice.

We have walked the path of effort, struggle, and willpower for years. This way of living feels so natural to us that effortless living feels like an impossible challenge. It's the reason why we often have a persistent feeling that says, "I have changed superficially, but deep down I am still the same and I don't know what to do about it." That fundamental change we seek points towards being able to live without exerting, yearning, craving, grasping, or reaching. It offers no guarantees of any kind either. It doesn't say, "Let go and your problems will be solved." We just don't know. All we know is effort is not the answer. There is real uncertainty involved.

This decision point is not new to us. Each one of us, comes right to the brink of it and then turns around. We go back to our old ways of resistance. Why do we retreat? Why do we run away? We do so because we come face to face with a powerful fear – the fear of the unknown. It says, *"What will happen if I let go of control? What if I fail?."* Being unable to face this fear we fall back. Then, after a few months or years when our problems become unbearable again, we find ourselves knocking on the same door, asking the same question: *"How do I let go?"* If we want to resolve this problem once and for all, we must get past this fear that stands guard.

Fear of the unknown

This time let's examine this fear instead of running away from it. What does the word *unknown* actually mean? For instance, can the mind really fear something which is not known? Can we fear threats we have never heard or known about? We can't. We can only fear something that we know, or have seen. In other words, when we say, *"I am afraid of the unknown"*, what we actually mean is, *"I am afraid of my past fear or pain returning."*

For instance, let's assume that we are considering leaving our job and starting our own business. We have done neither of these things before and yet we fear taking the plunge. This is what we call the *unknown*. What we truly fear is feeling insecure, uncertain or lost again. We can't know any of those feelings unless we have experienced them before in some other form. Only a person who has felt insecurity can imagine or remember what it feels like. Therefore, our *unknown* is a modified version of the *known* (the past) which we fear. Why does this verbal distinction matter?

It matters because when we perceive a lack of information about our future, we fill that void with our memories and label it the fear of the unknown. This label, 'unknown' protects the fear from being exposed. If we see that true unknown can't be feared, then we become more willing to enter it. We switch from, *"I fear what will happen"* to *"Let's see what happens."* Sometimes this small shift is all that is needed for us to try a different way of living.

The opposite side of this *fear of the unknown*, is the fear of losing the known. We are afraid to leave the comfort and the relative peace of mind which we currently enjoy. As J. Krishnamurti, Indian speaker and writer once said, *"We don't fear the unknown, we fear the loss of the known."* What is strange about this is that the '*known*' that we are clinging to is often the source of our suffering. It is misery in the disguise of comfort. In that example, the job we are afraid to leave is perhaps the main source of our frustration. Yet it gives us solace through familiarity, and seems preferable to entering the unknown.

Some of us understand all this and are prepared to let go of effort. If we have tried *hard* all our life, we become willing to try *easy*. We begin to relax in the face of uncertainty and consciously reduce the amount of striving behind our actions. As we do so and make slow progress, we begin to run into another problem. We realize that struggling has become so ingrained in us that even before we consciously know it, we are fighting our unresolved fears, hurts and desires. The Backwards Law is already in effect with the first breath we draw in the morning. We are resisting at the very core of our existence. By the time we become consciously aware that we are resisting, it is already too late. Then we struggle to let go and fall back into the old trap once again. So then how do we proceed when we have no conscious control over our resistance? How can we end that which is beyond our control?

The precipice

This subconscious conflict – between an attempt to let go and the conditioned desire to hold on – is the most crucial aspect of our journey. This back and forth is also a reason why most of us turn away at this juncture. We can't stand on this precipice. We're too afraid and we turn back. Yet a few of us are neither willing to go back, nor do we know how to go forward. We're stranded. The key to the change we seek seems so close, and yet just out of reach. As such, the only thing to be done is to remain in this place of *not-knowing as long as we can*. We reached here after questioning *everything* we knew, so we know this must be the right place to be. Though we don't have any more answers. We have reached the end of our knowledge. We have exhausted our understanding.

Finding Awareness

On the one hand is our will to find a breakthrough, and on the other is our utter inability to do so. Our unstoppable will now faces an insurmountable obstacle. This is the state of mind in which all our energy begins to gather in order to break through. Our mind enters a state of unshakeable concentration. It summons every ounce of mental energy it has, but since the obstacle is unscalable, that energy has nowhere to go. It continues to build up in place. This process of intensification pushes the mind deeper into itself than it ever has. It begins to shed all desires, fears, beliefs and even hope. Nothing exists apart from the enormity of the problem. The sky begins to darken, one last time.

To each one of us, this state appears differently. For some, it may appear in the form of facing a particular fear, addiction or hurt. To some it may appear in the form of guilt or sorrow. The question may take many forms: *"How am I to live with myself?"; "I am nobody without him, how am I to let go?"; "I am facing death because of this illness. How can I face death?"* The ways in which this crisis comes varies, but the *state of the mind it creates doesn't*. It has this same quality of dualistic inward forces approaching an end.

We can only recognize this period once it has passed, not while or before we are going through it. If we are facing such a situation and wonder whether we have arrived at the precipice, it creates another expectation, another glimmer and the mind gets distracted from the problem. The hope of coming out on top, prevents accumulation of energy. It is only when hope ceases to be a factor, does this assimilation finish and the me-thought becomes willing to admit that it has failed. Some call it rock-bottom, for the descent has ended. There is nothing beneath this. This is the end.

Then what is one to do? *You see, what can one do now? Everything* has been tried and done. All possible actions are complete. This realization is not conscious, but at levels deep within the mind. It can't be described or put into words. When the core of who we are realizes that there is *nothing else to be done,* the mind becomes untethered from its attachment to effort. It abandons action at all levels of being. The self takes a long time to come to this point. This is why it is important to be patient and persistent as we approach the precipice. If we escape out of fear, we never reach the edge. We never give our ego an opportunity to achieve its sacred failure.

This is why we can't trick ourselves into it. We can't plan or predict it. We can't pretend that we have already passed this stage. The pretense only adds to the frustration and the buildup. It is a part of our struggle towards that cliff. In other words, the very concept of applying effort to achieve a result begins to crumble. The path we are on begins to disintegrate in front of our own eyes. Every path, even if it's an exploration, implies a destination, a traveler and a journey. It implies a gradual progress, over time. Only when the tools of logic and reason break, are we prepared to understand what lies ahead.

Effort, trying, and control have absolutely no meaning when our mind reaches this place. The old chains are broken and there is nothing to replace them. There is a lightness and freedom. The opposing forces of the obstacle and the will dissipate each other, and neither remain. The fall begins. We become okay with whatever happens. We have passed into the unknown. When all inward action has ceased, the mind enters the *gate beyond all gates*. It is prepared for the final insight – the state of surrender.

29
Surrender

Only those who accept their fate, are given the power to change it.

The state of surrender is reached when we understand that there is nothing to be done. We realize that the more we resist the past, the stronger it becomes. So we begin to accept it, and the more we accept, it seems to weaken. Our ego begins to see its own fears, hurts, and desires as extensions of itself, instead of being separate entities that it must manipulate. They are made of the same tether, and they deserve this space as much as the ego does. Trying to control them is like controlling fire with fire. It can't be done. Our fears, pains and desires can't be destroyed, transformed or transcended. *They are us*. Anything we do to them only inflames the conflict within ourselves. This is the state of surrender and only absolute failure brings the ego to this realization. It is not verbal, at the level of thinking, but subconscious, at the level of feeling.

When this realization is complete, the ego-identity surrenders to an unresolved fear, pain, or a desire. The *'me-thought'*, which we saw in the chapter on ego, ends all its activity. It becomes still. This creates deep inner peace. The state of surrender alters our relationship with the dark aspects

Finding Awareness

of our ego. It brings together the shadow and the light, and merges them. This end of conflict brings about an immediate and an irreversible change in our minds. For instance, if we surrender to a fear, our *resistance to that fear* comes to an end. We no longer consider fear something to avoid. Our mind becomes okay with experiencing it. As such, the consequences which the fear threatened us with, lose their power. Suddenly, we are able to say, *"It's okay if I lose my job,"* or *"It's okay if I am unable to fight this addiction,"*; *"It's okay if I don't heal from this pain."* As we say those things, our peace only deepens.

Those fearful thoughts can come and go as they please, without the *'me-thought'* ever standing in their way. In essence, our fears lose their leverage over us. They transform into fearlessness. The pain, when allowed, becomes passion. It inflames and inspires the mind. A desire when allowed frees the mind from its clutches. It brings liberation. This is the transformation we had been waiting for.

Most of us expect freedom to be devoid of fears, pains, or desires, which is hardly the case. Freedom or transformation are only devoid of a conflict with those things.

This freedom and transformation appear when the mind let's go of every subconscious desire to change itself.

How and why does this happen? To understand this we must look at what Surrender involves. Even though it is a single word, it appears to be a combination of two processes – both of which happen simultaneously: non-interference and resolution.

Non-interference

The first thing we experience during this state is an unwillingness to interfere in whatever is unfolding. For the first time in our lives, we become a truly impartial observer. Until now, we felt a hidden desire to bring about some form of change in our inner or outer environment. Every time a fear or a desire would rise, we would interfere with it and get caught up in resistance. The resistance would then empower the pattern and help to keep it unresolved. The cycle would repeat for years on end. When there is this state of spontaneous non-interference, we stop refusing the thing which is coming up. We leave it alone. Our unresolved past now begins to surface.

As the old patterns arise, they look first for psychological resistance from us. When they find the *'me-thought'* to be quiet, they begin to look for physical resistance. They look for tension or stress in our body. Any physical tightness is enough for the patterns to cause resistance. However, as our minds and bodies are connected, our body surrenders too. It enters a state of deep repose. The pressure built up in our muscles – from years of resistance – begins to leave. As our body feels lighter, our peace deepens. The old patterns find nothing to grasp as they arise. They only find space and emptiness.

Resolution

This is the process of resolution. It begins the moment we refuse to interfere. Non-interference and resolution happen together. Whether it's a fear, an addictive pattern, or a hurt, we are now able to experience it fully. The unresolved past arises and begins to complete itself. This process can last for days or months once the state of surrender has happened. This long process can be intense for some of us, and quiet for others, but in every case our mind remains in a state of endless patience. From time to time, old memories come up and flash before our eyes but the 'me thought' steps away and lets it all unfold. Sometimes these flashbacks may invoke physical reactions. Yet, our mind is effortlessly focused on taking no action whatsoever. It refuses to interfere no matter what comes up.

This process resolves all our suffering and leaves us renewed and healed. The mind and the body feel cleansed and regenerated, like a rainforest after a thunderstorm. There is peace, stillness and quiet in our days. A new life begins.

With this, we have answered the third and the last question from the end of Chapter 12: What should be done with experiences that can't be resolved? We surrender to them, for then they resolve themselves. Once surrender happens, it triggers a cascade of profound and irreversible shifts in both our inner and outer lives. Changes that seemed impossible, now seem inevitable.

Presence

One of the first changes we see is, the state of *being*, now becomes more important than *becoming*. Our mind frequently stops looking for anything other than what *is*. Mental peace becomes the most important thing. We now *know that* the present moment has far more to offer than the past or the future. We spontaneously begin to practice presence. We understand the seduction of thinking, yet we value stillness more.

When being present becomes more important, the pressure to succeed melts away too, for success is an idea of the future. When we are no longer attached to success, we no longer fear failure either. Both success and failure seem irrelevant. They become an afterthought. What matters is living without any pressure or fear, whatsoever.

Power

This is why those who find this state of surrender also become, in some sense, headstrong. For they exist in a state of persistent refusal of the pressures society puts on them. They reject every single plan others have for them. So an inward state of surrender appears often as a state of outward rebellion. The more surrendered inwardly we become, the more revolutionary the outward personality becomes. This is the birth of our personal power and authenticity.

With no outward or inward pressure, all mental blockages dissolve. This brings freedom and inspiration. We now take the hardest of decisions with clarity and poise. Significant outer shifts happen as a result. We feel as if nothing stands in our way, should we decide to move in any particular direction. If we want we can choose to have goals, if not, we can choose to live without them. Either way, *we* decide. There is a deep stillness along with a vast potential for action. It becomes easy to do the things we once found impossible, for no one is standing in our own way, least of all, ourselves. The self-sabotage is over. In other words, we stumble upon the secret of effortless living.

Effortlessness

This effortlessness makes us feel as if our actions are *happening*, as much as we are *taking* them. Since the burden to perform is no more, we begin to relax in our daily life. We notice that the more we relax, the more control we seem to have. In other words, the less we grasp for control, the more control we find. We have a deep realization that only those who accept their fate, seem to find the power to change it. We are able to release our grip over our lives and let go. We find endless patience. We feel as if we could spend a whole lifetime taking a single breath. Everything seems easy. Especially the hardest things from the past, seem the easiest.

Flow

Surrender, in this way, becomes effortless control. It creates a stillness in movement or a movement in stillness. If we are in a state of surrender, we take far more actions than when we aren't. We accomplish far *more* in the outer world in far *less* time. We can fail or succeed as many times as we need without attaching to either state. *We remain in a state of flow in which we act until it's time to surrender and surrender, until it's time to act.* When progress becomes difficult, we learn to surrender and be patient. Then ideas and inspiration appear. When they do, we take actions based on them and progress happens. When the obstacles increase, we surrender again.

Finding Awareness

> Even though the initial experience of surrender is an event out of our control, once it happens, it can be practiced.

Our mind knows what it feels like and is able to access it during difficult life-situations. The more we practice surrender, the more it becomes a skill. We begin to get intimations of when to Surrender, and when to act. If the resistance we feel has a familiar intensity to it, we realize we are caught up in fighting, so we retreat and relax. Later, when we have an inspiring idea, we immediately act. Life becomes an endless state of flow, guided by our intuition.

As we saw in Chapter 24: The one self, self-awareness creates integration within the ego-identity. Surrender, however, brings integration to the entire structure of the ego. It heals the deep fragmentation we feel within and makes us whole. It takes away our desire to *change*, and gives us the power to *accept*. It frees enormous amounts of energy and liberates us from our past. In doing so, it converts our insecurity into security, our fears into fearlessness, and our pain into our passion. It completes our shift from comparison to learning, from loneliness to connection, from anger to forgiveness and from violence to compassion.

Self-discovery

We now see that our path is a circle, and that the end brings us back where we started. Our journey concludes by surrendering to our reality and therefore fundamentally transforming it. It shows us who we are *supposed to be* is exactly *who we already are*, for they are both one and the same. All we have to do is find out who we are, and then be that person, wholly. Then we can create a life where surrender and control exist in balance, and such a life brings harmony to everything it touches. It overflows with passion and holds nothing back for itself. Therefore, unbeknownst to it, like a flower facing into the sun, it becomes a source of endless beauty, strength and *love*.

Questions and Answers

Over the past two years, I have had countless conversations with my Instagram followers, which inspired me to capture all the insights, lessons and experiences in this book. People seeking answers trusted me with their deepest concerns as they sought to find meaning and understanding within themselves. Many of those questions complement the work we have already done, so I wanted to share them with you as well. They are divided into seven sub-topics: self-awareness, self-acceptance, relationships, meditation, surrender, ego and goals.

I hope that some of these questions echo the unanswered queries you might have.

Self-Awareness

- **How do you remind yourself to stay aware of your thoughts/feelings as a regular habit?**

    Awareness is a skill that takes practice. Initially, it feels like one has to try to be actively aware to look inwards. Yet with practice, it becomes a reflex, like a muscle memory. After a while, we don't practice awareness; it just begins to happen. It goes from being active observation to passive. When an out-of-the-ordinary thought or situation arises, awareness instantly catches it. It's like a filter that looks for emotional responses or triggers. When those triggers happen, we notice them effortlessly.

It's not helpful to practice active awareness all the time since it quickly becomes exhausting. Self-awareness then becomes an additional problem in life. It may be better to be oblivious of one's triggers, than be actively aware and miserable. If we understand this, then we let this practice of watching it sink into the subconscious mind where it does its job without becoming another problem to solve.

- **I lose awareness when I am at work, but I practice well when I am alone. How do I keep my awareness at all times?**

    This happens because our connection between our body and mind isn't that strong. It can only be felt when there is no challenge while we are in the comfort of our homes. When that connection is intensified, we can feel it all the time, even when we are among people who we find difficult.

- **How to overcome feelings of meaninglessness in life?**

    By giving up the search for meaning and finding something that you love to do, then doing it for a long time. The more things you love, the better.

    Eventually one of them will become a passion. Then one of those passions may feel like a responsibility. When your passion meets responsibility, it becomes your purpose. And your purpose will provide you the meaning you seek.

- **I am feeling stuck. What do I do?**

    Stop trying so hard. Try easy.

    Trying *hard* is what gets us stuck. Trying *easy* shows us how to flow.

- **How do you build awareness and hold the version of who you want to become without forcing it?**

    When you build awareness, it will help you clear the house. It will help you discard all the old furniture that you keep bumping into while walking around. It will make space for you. When that space grows, you will naturally want to bring in new things into that space, but this time, you will be more careful. You'll want to create a version of this house that aligns with your intuition and drifts. You will want to do things which you love. This process is seamless. Understanding oneself leads one into discovering the things that they truly love. Forcing of any kind indicates that somewhere things aren't clear.

    If you already know what you want to do, then all you have to do is move in that direction. Progress may be difficult if we aren't fully clear or committed to our path. A few obstacles are enough to throw us off. So the most important thing is finding clarity about who we want to become. That clarity is everything. It is self-knowledge itself. It answers the question, *"Why am I putting myself through all this?"* Once we have that 'why' answered, we can keep walking our path no matter how difficult it gets. Friedrich Nietzsche said, *"He who has a why to live, can bear with almost any how."*

Finding Awareness

- **How do you maintain awareness around people who challenge our awareness?**

    The answer is hidden in the question itself. They challenge our awareness, so the only response is more awareness. The deeper the connection we have with ourselves, the less other people's psychological state affects us. The responsibility for our state of mind is our responsibility and no one else's.

    It's a good practice to wait to be triggered by someone so you can test your inward connection. If you keep hurtling down the same old reactions of fear or anger, then the work remains undone.

- **Can you talk more about watching 'negative' thoughts and not getting attached?**

    Thoughts aren't negative or positive. They are just thoughts. We have divided our inner world into positive and negative. Try and see them from a neutral point of view and you'll get a glimpse into the underlying emotions, feelings and memories that are creating those thoughts.

    We get attached to those thoughts because we judge them as wrong and want to dissolve them. That intent to destroy those thoughts begins a battle with them, and anything we inwardly fight makes it stronger. Reconsider your approach to resisting the negative and ask yourself if you can invest some more time in simply understanding, rather than criticizing your inner world. That is the way of freedom.

- **How do I stop procrastinating?**

    If we are serious about getting something done, the hours in the day are not enough. However, procrastination is a sign that we lack seriousness about reaching the objective. We have a goal but we also perhaps have a belief that we can't achieve it. Fear of failure can also masquerade as procrastination. The mind thinks, *"If I don't even try, I will have a great excuse for failing."* When we really commit to our goals, there is no such thing as procrastination. There is only clarity and a force that pulls us towards our objective. In effect, procrastination is not a real problem. It is an illusory side effect of confusion. The real problem, if you can call it that, is the lack of clarity about what we want and whether we truly want it.

- **How do I learn to express my thoughts?**

    There is no such thing as inability to express one's thoughts. There is however a lack of awareness about what we are thinking. Inability to *see* becomes the inability to *describe*. When we can see our thoughts clearly, we are able to describe them. However, when we are confused and unsure about what we are thinking, we have a fear of being judged or misunderstood. This fear blocks us from clear expression. Learning how to express fearlessly is the same thing as figuring out what we must express. Then the rest unfolds naturally.

- **How do I stop overthinking?**

    Overthinking happens for two reasons. One is fear and the other is confusion. Getting to the root of what one is afraid of resolves both these problems. It creates silence.

    For instance if we are afraid of not living up to the expectations of the world, we get caught up in figuring out ways to achieve that objective. This is overthinking. The mind tries to cover every contingency by planning possible solutions in advance. To accept this fear and confusion creates a calmness in thinking. It temporarily resolves the conflict within. It ends overthinking.

Another way to calm the mind is to practice centering meditations of conscious breathing, listening, seeing and feeling. They help us connect with the wordless reality and bring peace to the mind.

- **How do you deal with overanalyzing the past and feeling those emotions repeatedly?**

To *let it go* is to *let it be*. To *let it be* is to *let it come*.

This means the past is not analyzed as much as observed and allowed. If this observation gets overwhelming, take a break. If we are too eager to heal, it takes longer. A helpful mindset is that of curiosity and interest in understanding one's past. That curiosity makes this process of understanding one's own suffering a little more bearable. Our past isn't going anywhere so take your time, breathe and be patient with yourself. How long does it take? The more time you make for it, the less time it takes for the past to arise and resolve. The less time we make for it, the longer it takes.

Understand the process of allowing unresolved memories and emotions to resolve themselves. Sometimes it takes an insight for it to happen; sometimes there is no answer and only acceptance remains. Once those unresolved emotions are settled, they lose their charge, their power. Learn the art of being patient, being aware and not interfering with the pain as it flows through you. Like a dark cloud, it will come and pass. Only when we resist this process, do we push the rising pain back inside, and make it stronger. If we don't want to feel them repeatedly, we have to stop resisting how they make us feel. The fastest way is through. Let them arise and see if you can be still as they do.

- **How can I be highly focused and calm at the same time?**

    High focus and calm go together; desperation and calm don't. The first thing we can try is doing whatever we are about ten percent slower. This slowing down relaxes the mind and helps it find flow. The slower we go, the less pressure we feel. The less pressure, we feel the faster we go. This is flow. So slowing down is the key to finding this state, which contains both focus and calm.

    Things get even easier when we are doing something we love. Then flow is natural. There is little to no strain in doing our work, yet the work gets done, and creatively too. We are taught to struggle to get what we want, yet struggle only leads to more struggle. Instead of trying to find focus, it's better to seek this flow. If we find focus through straining, we struggle to maintain calmness along with it. If we can find focus through flow, then calmness is already a part of it.

- **Do willpower and awareness complement each other?**

    Willpower is needed to accomplish a goal. Awareness is required to know if that goal is worth accomplishing. Therefore, willpower without awareness can take us down the wrong path. We need self-awareness to find the right path, then willpower to follow that path. With self-awareness, it becomes possible to find one's drifts. Drifts are the things which we are naturally inclined to do well. When we pick a drift and want to achieve a certain level of skill in it, we require willpower to keep going. That's the only role willpower plays. It helps us go in the right direction with more focus. When willpower is exhausted and we get stuck, then self-awareness reminds us to *'try easy'* instead of *'trying hard'*. It shows us how to start flowing, so that we become efficient and conserve willpower as we progress. This way, they both work together, always maintaining a balance in movement, never exhausting each other.

- **What helps to reduce boredom?**

    Curiosity. Being curious about the world and reading about it takes care of boredom. We are bored because we don't find that many things interesting, often because we haven't looked deeply enough, even at the things we claim to love. Boredom, laziness, lethargy are signs that indicate a lack of inspiration, a lack of beauty in living. When we see something subtle and elegant, we perceive beauty. And that perception of beauty inspires us. Boredom therefore is a sign that we are operating at a level of superficiality, for everything seems obvious and uninteresting.

    Boredom is an indicator that we aren't functioning at our full potential, therefore it's a cause for celebration. It means growth is still possible. Curiosity, observation and continuous learning keep boredom at bay. There are millions of good books out there. How many of them have we read? There are so many art forms out there. How many have we tried our hand at? The world is incredibly complex and bewildering. Constant learning keeps us connected to the beauty of life and away from boredom.

- **What is happiness?**

    Happiness isn't pleasure or comfort. It can come out of intense effort too. When our effort is in the direction of the thing we love doing, it creates a byproduct called happiness. It is not in the fruit of our labor, but in the laboring itself. The result is secondary. The process is primary. However when we are concerned with pleasure in the name

Questions and Answers

of happiness, the result becomes primary, and the process secondary.

For instance, if our goal is to be a millionaire, or to be on the cover of a magazine, the road to those leads through misery, if not ours, then someone else's. When the means don't matter as much as the end, it becomes easy to trample everything in our path to get what we want. This attachment to the goal leads to great suffering. Happiness comes when that attachment is over, and the love of the process begins. Happiness is an unexpected consequence of doing something we find meaningful. It sneaks up on those who aren't looking for it.

- **How do you find inner balance in everyday life?**

By taking the time to connect with oneself every day. We feel connected when we perceive our mind and body together. This happens through a meditation technique, vigorous exercise or any means that take our attention inward. With consistent practice, we are able to find the balance. When life throws us a curveball, instead of reacting to it, our attention goes inwards and we respond to the challenge. This becomes a new pattern.

We begin to rely more and more on the internal state of harmony which is able to meet any challenge we face, as opposed to unconsciously reacting based on old, conditioned behaviors. When we act from the present moment this way, we feel balanced.

- **How do I process emotions like anger?**

We rarely get angry at an infant or a child for misbehaving. Why? Because we know they aren't aware of what they are doing and that's why we can process and respond to their behavior properly. We stay in charge of ourselves and the situation. We know we are in control.

What happens when adults do or say something that makes us angry? Their actions denigrate something we value: our reputation, our self-respect or our self-image. In other words, *we* begin to lose control of the situation. Anger then arises to (violently) snatch that control back from them. In both cases, someone acted wrongly, but only in the second case did we lose control over ourselves. So anger is never because of someone else; it's because of our inability to respond to the challenge they create. If we never lost control of ourselves or the situation, we would never have gotten angry.

For instance, a good martial artist practices to be in stressful situations and maintain a calm state of mind. So, a situation that causes anger in an untrained person, creates focus and alertness in a trained fighter, for she has trained not to lose control. Anger, in that sense, is always aimed at ourselves, for losing that control. It has got nothing to do with the other person. We get triggered by our own helplessness. The instant we know how to respond to a person's challenge, we don't get angry. Therefore, our work lies in understanding how to respond.

Find out exactly what makes you upset. Is it that we are unable to make others see us as we see ourselves and that makes us angry? Are we invested in others seeing us exactly as we want them to? Why can't we let them think whatever they want? What are we so afraid of? In investigating these questions, we find the answer.

Questions and Answers

- **What transformation can we achieve with breath awareness?**

    Breath awareness tells us about our mental state. If we are nervous, anxious, afraid, or angry, our breathing is shallow and rapid. If we are aware of our breath, it can warn us of a fear or stress building up in the depths of our subconscious mind. We can catch the problem before it blows out of proportion.

    Breath awareness is also helpful if the problem does blow up and we lose control of our mind. Controlling the breath, then bringing it back to our resonance frequency, is an indirect and good way of gaining short-term control. Long-term control is, of course, a different matter. Our resonance frequency varies. It is when we take about five to seven breaths per minute in a calm, easy manner and feel the mental fog clear. A good breath is one which isn't too deep nor too shallow. This pattern temporarily clears our emotions and brings clarity in the mind. With practice of breath awareness, our breathing can become an anchor for our state of mind. In stressful situations we can focus on our breathing and try to regulate it, rather than controlling our thoughts. This way we can indirectly control our inner states. In other words, breathing is the way out of our problems.

- **Do you do affirmations? When do you use them, and when do you not?**

    At every stage in our process, we use different tools to make progress. However, as I got older, I realized that there are certain mechanistic things which can be achieved using positive thinking, affirmations and other methods. For instance, if you want to pass a competitive exam, get a job

245

in a company, make your sales targets, or achieve other practical things at work, then these methods of motivating oneself through positive affirmations could be useful. If I need to find a job, and I have no money to pay the bills, there is no time to practice self-awareness and meditation to find the long-term answers. That is not a luxury affordable to us in a desperate situation. We need to act, and act now. This is when these practical tools, like affirmations, can help us rise from a temporary problem.

However, if our problem involves changing the mind of our partner, then these methods don't work. You can't will someone else into loving you back or changing their behavior. When human relationships, fear, suffering, trauma, or addictions are involved, affirmations and positive thinking don't work. In fact, they usually backfire. If you are trying to get over a painful separation, affirmations are not the right answer. This is where self-awareness, acceptance and surrender reveal the path ahead for you.

- **How do we discern between manifesting our purpose and a craving?**

    I don't like the word *manifesting*. Let's call it *moving in the direction of your true calling* or *purpose*. Our purpose has a sense of being irrefutable. We have no choice in the matter. It is quite beyond our personal pursuit of pleasure. It is larger than us. It feels as if there is beauty and love associated with it. It feels as if the doing is the reward, not some end goal. A craving usually shows up as an end goal and creates a battle between desire and fear. A craving is an attachment. One moment is full of desire and one full of fear.

    A *calling* feels calm and steady. It has a warm glow to it. It does not flicker. It may create anxiety and fear too, but we feel pulled towards this experiencing fear, not away from it. There is no inward travail that comes with a craving or attachment. A calling or a purpose comes with a steady buildup of energy over many years. It doesn't go away.

However, if we become attached to our calling, talk endlessly or brag about it, then it becomes a craving. Attachment always brings some form of suffering. When our identity gets tangled with our purpose, it has become a craving. We have lost our way. If we can let go and walk away from it, then that craving can again transform back into our purpose. If we try to possess a truth, it turns into a lie. If we acknowledge a lie, it turns into a truth.

- **Why do people judge?**

    Because it's easy. Understanding is difficult and requires patience. It requires one to be in a state of not knowing. Therefore, we are always trying to mentally 'place' people. Once we can place them, it makes us feel as if we know how to deal with them. Judging creates an illusion of knowledge and security.

- **Is it good to be a sensitive person?**

    One has to become highly sensitive to understand the human mind. Insensitivity only makes us overlook the important things. To be sensitive is to see as much as possible, without getting dragged into it. Sensitivity implies care, watchfulness, love, compassion, beauty, and everything in between. There is a balance in being emotionally sensitive, yet not being overwhelmed by other's emotions. Sensitivity has to be centered and grounded. When it is ungrounded, then it mixes someone else's pain with our own. The end result is just more pain.

Finding Awareness

To feel someone else's pain, but also feel one's own centeredness is to find that balance. That way, we can't be consumed by someone else's pain. We may cry with them, but we still will have access to our own inner peace. That is the kind of compassion that can heal, for it is capable of feeling, yet not losing oneself in it. Sensitivity is a gift when it is channeled properly. It is the only tool we have to fathom the depths of human suffering, beauty and life.

- **Is it hard to keep clarity when we are ill?**

Yes. Illness is a time to take rest. It is not the time to be demanding clarity from oneself. When we get back to our healthy selves, we can pick up where we left off. There is no hurry. Take your time. Let the body take its time.

However, if our illness is severe, then it gives us the opportunity to open the doorway of surrender. Surrender doesn't mean we give up the desire to live, it only means we know how to flow with life.

- **How do you navigate scarcity mindset and the anxiety of the unknown? I want to manifest abundance. How do I do it?**

The fear of the unknown doesn't exist. What exists is fear of the unpleasant known (past) repeating in the future. Truly facing the unknown creates no fear whatsoever. It creates open-ended curiosity, which is a big part of human nature. The unknown is blank and empty. We tend to fill it up with fear, which is from our past, and call it the unknown. The real question is, how to deal with fear itself? By not being afraid of it. Letting it come and go as it pleases. Fear isn't the real problem; fear *about the fear*, is. Surrender, then you won't be afraid of being afraid. Then fear will become something which is natural and normal. It will come and go as it pleases without dragging you along.

Why do we want to manifest abundance? Isn't that fanciful idea a product of a mind which is struggling with fear and scarcity? If so, then that idea must be purely imaginary. Abundance can't be imagined. If it can be, then it has no real value apart from making oneself comfortable and, therefore, remaining unchanged. Abundance is the lack of self-imposed barriers. It is to feel free from within, without any force or imagination manufacturing it. One can't feel that freedom, that lack of frontiers, if one is constantly fighting oneself. If I am fighting *my fear, my insecurity* or *my hurts*, I and myself are in conflict. Therefore, there is no such thing as real abundance, or freedom unless one has surrendered to one's reality. There is only the scarcity, conflict and fear, along with a pacifying idea of imaginary abundance.

If one has surrendered, one has ended that battle between me and myself. One has become whole. If we can do it even once, then a tremendous amount of energy becomes available to us, for it is no longer being wasted in inward conflict. That energy alone is abundant, endless and comes in vast inexhaustible reserves.

Self-Acceptance

- **How do I find self-love?**

    Many of us are caught in this struggle to find self-love. In its pursuit, we do various things like asserting ourselves, saying "no" to others, building strong boundaries, protecting our mental state, avoiding certain people, etc. All these things are fair, except they don't approach the problem directly but in a roundabout way. Self-love isn't a thing to chase. If it is pursued, one is always at the risk of toeing the line between self-love and self-justification, between self-respect and ego. Self-love, if there is such a thing, is a quiet side effect of something else altogether. That thing is having a strong inward connection with oneself, without any distortion or desires. Distortion happens when we want to change what we observe in ourselves. I'm too weak, confused, emotional or I have too much empathy or whatever it may be. This is hard to avoid because judgments (or labels) are automatic. But once a judgment happens, the mind wants to change itself in some way or another (increase the good and reduce the bad qualities). That desire to change creates distortion. Why? Because we have stopped paying attention to what *is* and have started to run behind what *should be*. Staying with *what is,* is to be connected with oneself. This is enough. Not changing oneself, but simply knowing oneself. Isn't that easier?

Once we have this connection, which is when we can notice the slightest change in our emotional states, our feelings or our thoughts. We begin to rest more and more in our own skin. This relaxation makes us want to be with ourselves. It makes us gently align with our goals and values. This alignment is nothing but self-love.

It's a serendipitous discovery, a happy accident of being connected and integrated from within. This connection is the answer to almost every problem that arises in our life or the lives of our loved ones. For when we are connected we can respond without hesitation, fear or confusion. We're always there, in the moment, where everything else is.

- **How do you overcome self-criticism?**

    Self-criticism is a sign that we are caught up in comparing ourselves with others or some imagined ideal. Upon finding that we aren't good enough, we judge ourselves. Covering up self-criticism with self-praise or self-love is not the right approach. If we do so, we create more inward conflict. The question to ask is, *"Why am I comparing myself with someone else?"* We compare because sometimes that's the only tool we have to measure ourselves. Through comparisons, we are asking the world to tell us who we are, for we don't know it ourselves. Harsh words said to us in our childhood, or even cultural pressures while growing up, could lead to this habit. But this habit can be broken.

    Turning all comparison into learning is how this can be ended. Learning not just about oneself, which is self-awareness, but also about the world. Reading more, mastering a skill, building something from scratch is how we learn. It slowly takes our mind away from comparison and towards the habit of learning. We begin to enjoy our own company. When we focus on learning, we take our attention away from criticism and towards enjoyment and improvement. Knowledge about the world and ourselves also makes us more secure. When we feel safe and secure with who we are, we stop asking others. Come to think of it, this is the answer we were looking for.

- **How do I get over the fear of being judged?**

    The simple answer is by instantly knowing whether that judgment is true or false. If it's true, there is nothing to be worried about. If it's false, what's there to worry about? If true, we improve ourselves. If false, we ignore it and keep moving forward.

We fear that someone's judgment could be true, only when we are blindsided by it, only because we hadn't examined the same thing about ourselves before. If we have done the work of understanding ourselves, then very few judgments can catch us off-guard. We have seen everything. There is little else someone else can teach us about ourselves, that we already don't know. Yet, sometimes people are right. When we are humble and honest in our search, a negative judgment from someone can become a cause for celebration. It means we still have more work to do, and we always welcome an opportunity to grow. So we get over the fear of being judged by looking deeper at who we are in reality.

- **How do I stop seeking validation?**

    What's important is not the validation we seek, but the deficiency we feel before we seek it. Where does it come from? It comes from two places. First, from our insecurity, and second, from a human being's genuine desire for connecting with others of its own kind. We can address both sources for they are related.

    Insecurity is the main reason we seek constant validation. Our insecurity makes us view others through suspicion, fear and doubt for we are always occupied with trying to protect ourselves. What hope do we have to connect with others if we can't be fearless and vulnerable in their presence? So insecurity starves the need for genuine connection with others. It creates this need for constant approval and validation seeking.

    We address this insecurity by developing unassailable self-knowledge. Which means knowing ourselves on our own terms. We have to connect with our bodies and learn the art of insight meditation. We have to question all our beliefs, both positive and negative. We must leave no stone unturned in our inner landscape. When we know ourselves with precision we are also able to describe our feelings and emotions precisely. Having learned both listening and expressing along our inner journey, now we are able to form inseparable bonds with people in our lives. It fulfills the core and natural desire we all have to be accepted and loved by fellow humans.

When our root desire for connection is fulfilled, seeking validation fades away, for we already received it. Not only do we have our own validation through self-knowledge, but also the ability to create and foster loving relationships. We are fulfilled at all levels of being.

- **How do I deal with the fear of being lonely?**

    Fear of being alone exists when we don't know how to be with ourselves. When we are afraid of our own thoughts and don't understand them, it is natural to feel unpleasant in our own company. Whether just being alone in a new city, or temporarily being out of a relationship, loneliness is a good thing. That's when we have the opportunity to discover who we are. It is the only time when we can study ourselves without outside influences or distractions.

    Surely, we need interpersonal closeness, but how can we be close to someone else, if we can't stand ourselves? So the right approach is to engage in learning while we are alone – about oneself through meditation or art, and about the world through reading, exploring or practicing an art. Then solitude becomes not just enjoyable, but even desirable from time to time.

Finding Awareness

- **Can you talk about the topic of jealousy? I feel a lot of envy for a friend and feel like I am a bad person.**

    Jealousy is a very natural feeling. It can be seen even among animals. For example, chimpanzees show a very strong understanding of fairness. If they don't get the same treat for performing the exact same task, they get angry. Chronic comparison causes jealousy. If we are focusing on other people's lives, that means we are *ignoring* ours.

    Face it and feel it. Say to yourself, *"Okay I am feeling really jealous. That's interesting. Let me watch it for a while. Let me find out what thoughts it's making me think."* To a person who is working on herself, jealousy and hate are great entry points into oneself. They are powerful triggers that show us where we are unclear about our own feelings.

    When we examine jealousy we realize that if we want what they have, we can observe them, ask them questions, and learn from them. Jealousy is finished. If we don't want what they have, then there is no real reason to be jealous anyway, right? Feeling jealous is then simply a distraction our mind uses to avoid working on itself. Usually, it has a lot to work with– a lot to be thankful for, a lot to express gratitude for. Gratitude fills our heart with strength. Instead of being resentful for what someone else has, when we focus on being thankful for what we have, life becomes simple and beautiful. Then we can perhaps feel love for others.

- **How do you forgive yourself?**

    You don't. You only try to understand yourself. When that understanding reaches a certain point, you look back and realize that forgiveness has happened. That point arrives when we realize that we did what we did, because that is what the totality of our self-understanding made us do then. How do we know that? Because that's what we did. If we could have controlled our actions, we would have. Actions can't be controlled, for they arise seamlessly out of our self-knowing. Then we say, *"Perhaps I should have had more self-knowledge back then. I should have been more aware, then I could have acted differently."*

We can't control what our past selves knew. We can only control what our present self knows, and therefore does. Self-knowledge can only be gained in the present moment, which is what we are doing. This understanding of oneself in the present moment, is the only valid action to be taken, and we are taking it now. Changing the past is impossible. There is nothing to be done about it. Until this sinks into the subconscious mind, it keeps trying to change the past. When this unconscious attempt to change what happened falls away, so does the guilt. Then we can let the past go and forgive ourselves for what happened.

- **Will forgiving myself cause others to forgive me as well?**

Not necessarily, but it will make it much more likely. If we are guilt-ridden, then we speak from a place of self-doubt. All our actions betray this confusion we live under. If we doubt ourselves, how can someone else trust us? If they can't trust us, they feel as if we haven't changed, and therefore withhold forgiveness.

Seeking forgiveness is therefore the surest way to not receive it. The right path is to find that space in which we can forgive ourselves. The rest should take care of itself. When we 'seek' forgiveness it pins our ability to change behavior, on what others think about us. *"If he doesn't forgive me, what is the point in changing?"* asks our subconscious mind. It is better to ensure that the change we seek is primary and the forgiveness we desire is secondary. Then it becomes more likely that we will receive it.

Finding Awareness

- **How do I deal with large social gatherings? I feel anxious and nervous all the time.**

    Don't focus on the number of people there. Focus on the one person you're talking to. Notice how right now your attention is not on them, but on your fear and anxiety. Refocus that attention away from, *"What are people thinking about me?"* to *"What is this one person saying?"* Pay attention to the sensations and sounds around you. See how they are impersonal in nature. Notice how none of what is happening is referring to you personally, except your own mind. Observe everything. Relax and flow with the present. Be so intensely aware that your mental dialogue and imagination can't take hold. Give your complete attention to the one person in front of you.

    There's just one person in a social gathering anyway, just many times over.

- **I was raised in a religious house with strict traditions. My family forces me to act like them. What should I do?**

    Traditions are meant to bring people together, not control people based on fear. Traditions, when enforced, have no value. Our path calls us to find out what is the right action and develop the fearlessness to take it. If one wants to live in psychological freedom, challenging and flouting norms often comes with the territory. Yet, defying norms just for the sake of doing so has no meaning either. Abandoning one's religion or culture without understanding one's actions is the same as blindly conforming to them. We have to decide what kind of life we want to lead, and then live it. Everyone is on a different path. You could follow your religion or culture and yet be free of it. You could not follow them, and yet live a life of profound devotion. The choice is yours.

Questions and Answers

Relationships

- **How do you improve emotional bonding and emotional stability in relationships to connect at a deep level?**

    By taking the responsibility to improve ourselves, not our partner. We are often eager to change our partner, but that is impossible. We can't change another human being. The only thing we can do (barely) is change ourselves and hope that our partner may reciprocate. True change in ourselves is the *only* way we can inspire our partners to look at their own actions. Most of us find this difficult, because we are more eager to see them change, while keeping ourselves exactly the same.

    The primary thing is to change oneself and forget about what our partner may be doing for their emotional well-being. If and when the change in us is *real*, they notice it. It is impossible for them not to, for our behavior is completely transformed over a period of time. It is most powerful when they come to it naturally on their own. At that point, they become open to what we have to say. Our relationship begins to naturally deepen because we didn't force any such thing to happen. *The only way a deep connection happens is when each individual in a relationship is connected to themselves at a deep level. Then they can connect with their partner with the same intensity.* The good news is, only one person is required to go within, and the other follows, as long as the first one has no such expectations.

- **How do you fix a strained relationship?**

    We all know that being kind, caring and respectful towards our partner is important. The challenge lies in understanding how that is to be accomplished when we are triggered by something our partner does or says. The goal is not to react, but to respond to them. We do it through the right way of communication.

There are two parts to it: listening and expressing. Most of us listen while trying to speak or when we are lost in thought. Can we listen in such a way that we forget our own existence? If yes, then that is undivided or unconditioned listening. Such listening engages our conscious mind in the act of total presence, while the subconscious mind processes the words which we hear. When we respond, that response is now direct, honest and true to who we are. It is also devoid of fear or anger, because we never stoke our unresolved past. Such a response is articulate, kind and honest. It brings out the feelings of trust we have for our partner. It is full of compassion and love. When the violence within us ends, our relationships begin to heal.

- **I keep getting into a relationship with the same kind of people who hurt me the first time? Why is this happening?**

    If we don't know the real reasons why our previous relationship failed, how can we recognize them when they reappear? This is why we find ourselves going in circles. We have to question whether we misidentified the root cause the first time. We have to be willing to look deeper at what is happening. One of the major reasons appears to be that we pick the people who can fix our problems or fulfill our needs. Therein lies a major problem, for no one can truly resolve our issues and fulfill our needs but ourselves. Two broken cups can't be fixed with each other's pieces since they broke in different ways. They are made of different materials, shapes and sizes. They each have to become whole first. This means we have to take a journey into knowing ourselves before we hastily enter new relationships.

Without knowing ourselves, we can't identify what qualities in a human being complement our nature and which don't. We can't know our preferences, our likes or dislikes. So, what do we do? We just accept whoever comes along, based on superficial attributes, such as appearance or sexual compatibility, and just go along, while ignoring potential red flags of which we are only too willing to ignore. We desire security that comes from the comfort of a relationship. We are afraid of being alone.

It is far more important to know oneself deeply, than it is to be in a relationship. When we focus on understanding ourselves, our conditioning begins to dissolve and we begin to truly know who we are. Then we can know what we want in a relationship and look specifically for a set of attributes or traits that we value in our partners. Now, even if finding the right partner may take time, we avoid a great deal of pain, suffering and regret by avoiding relationships which may not be right for us. Now, not only do we become patient in our search, but also confident in our approach towards it. A deep and fulfilling relationship then, is a foregone conclusion. It is inevitable.

- **Should love hurt? If attachments also hurt, how can I tell the difference?**

    It depends on what we mean by that strange, overused word: love, for it is easily confused with attachment. Attachment creates suffering in relationships. When we become identified with the other person, their departure can create pain. However, love also creates pain. For instance, a mother suffers if her child is sick because she loves her

Finding Awareness

child. If the child grows up and doesn't make the cultural or religious choices the mother expects of her, then the mother suffers again, but this time, due to attachment. Attachment comes with expectations; love doesn't.

So, both love and attachment can cause suffering. *Only one of them is necessary.* The pain that comes when an attachment is broken is *me-centered*. It's not concerned with the happiness and well-being of another person, but of oneself. It also creates anger, regret and disappointment since it relates to an expectation being unfulfilled. This is unnecessary suffering.

The pain from love tends not to be focused on oneself, but on the person who is suffering. It is concerned primarily with their well-being. It creates no anger, regret or disappointment of any kind. It has no expectations that were broken. This is necessary suffering, for without it love or compassion couldn't exist. *To love is to be willing to share in someone else's pain.*

Attachment creates fear and control, while love creates vulnerability and care for another. Both cause suffering, but only one of them is unnecessary.

- **How do you understand being rejected in a relationship?**

Rejection is not about us. It's not even about them. It's about acknowledging the reality of what would have happened, if we had been accepted. It takes two people to believe in a happy future for a relationship to thrive. When one person doesn't think so, there may be a reason behind it that the other isn't able to see. So perhaps they saved us from more long-term pain. Being rejected later, after an initial acceptance would be much worse than this present rejection. This isn't rationalizing the pain, but to make space for others' opinions, and acknowledge that they sometimes see a truth, that we refuse to, or can't. In that sense they aren't rejecting us, but saving us from unnecessary suffering and for that, we should always be thankful. What of the pain that remains?

Pain is never the problem; our resistance to it is. It ceases to be pain when we accept and surrender to what happened. Sometimes, there are no answers.

- **How do I get over the fear of losing someone?**

    When we are afraid of losing someone, it suggests that our thoughts are more focused on losing them, than in being with them. If we are fully present with someone, totally there – which implies listening, caring for what they have to say, keeping up with them in every fleeting moment – does our mind have the time or energy to think about losing them? Of course not. It's only when our present experience with them is full of distractions does that fear creep in. That's when the relationship we have with them deteriorates. If we can be fully present, our mind has no time or space to feel the fear of losing them.

    Be so intensely present that you feel as if you can live a lifetime in each minute. Then that fear will never be able to touch you.

- **Can't I just move on if someone hurt me instead of forgiving the person?**

    Yes. We can forget and yet not forgive, or forgive and not yet forget. The latter is better. The emotional content of our memories matter more than the memories themselves. To forgive is to release (or resolve) that emotional content. The

Finding Awareness

memory itself is like an empty shell or a box. You can keep it or throw it away. It doesn't matter.

However, if we throw away the box before resolving the emotional content, then it spills over into other areas of our life. So we could forget a painful relationship, but that pain has consequences. Perhaps we develop trust issues with people without knowing where they are coming from. Perhaps we act out our past pain on our current partner for no fault of theirs.

It is important to give ourselves space and time to deal with the pain we feel. If there is no way to release it using meditation, then surrendering to it helps it rise up and eventually leave.

- **I have a deep fear of being cheated on even though my partner gives me no reason to doubt. Does this have something to do with my parents being divorced? How do I stop feeling this fear?**

By living in the moment, not in the past. We often see our current relationship through the lens of the conditioning that our parents passed on to us. Our past begins to judge our present. In some ways, this conditioning wants our partner to behave the way our parents did. When we have an argument with our partner, we find ourselves saying the same things which our parents said to each other when they fought. The parent who we mimic is the one who has successfully passed on their conditioning to us.

It makes us recreate that same energy we grew up with in our house. We feel comfortable there, even if it feels painful. So, we say things to our partners, accusing them of doing things our father or mother once did. They obviously have no clue as to what is inviting this, so they either withdraw

Questions and Answers

or fight back. Eventually, we get what our conditioning wants. We have now unknowingly created the same painful atmosphere that we grew up in.

Our mind, in its urge to feel the same old familiar pain, has glossed over the fact that our partner and our parents are completely different people. There is no real reason for *our partner* to act like one of our parents, but there is a reason for *us* to do so! We are our parent's children and the inheritors of their conditioning. So, the responsibility is ours, more than our partner's, to ensure that we live and breathe in the present moment and give them the full attention and love they deserve. It is our responsibility to extricate our mind out of our painful past and consciously create a future that we want.

- **You have said that expectations are a form of violence. How should I stop having expectations from my loved ones? It seems impossible to do.**

    Expectations are a part of any relationship. Some are fundamental, such as caring, communication, physical intimacy, etc. However, most other expectations come from our attachments. We want our partners to protect us emotionally, solve all our problems, pay attention to us all the time, make us a priority in their lives and so on. These are the reasons why our partners feel pressured and threatened with consequences in our relationship. To protect themselves, they become aloof or defiant, in turn reflecting that violence back to us.

    By becoming aware of these expectations, and letting them go one by one, we can let our partners be. This requires that we do the work necessary to become self-sufficient in the relationship. When we don't expect anything from our partners, they slowly feel free and accepted in our presence. When they perceive that the threat and pressure of our expectations has left, they let their guards down. They become more vulnerable and loving. They sometimes undergo the changes we originally wanted to see in them.

This doesn't mean we can *pretend* to not have expectations in order to influence a change in them, for that is still expectation. Their ego can see right through our act. Our conscious non-expectation has to be genuine and real, only then does it lead to healing in our relationships.

- **Why is it so easy to slip back into a pattern of codependency?**

    Because codependency is a symptom of a deeper problem – insecurity. Security is to know what is happening within. Insecurity is to not know what's inside our own mind. Imagine that you're living in a house with ten rooms, nine of which you have never entered. Will you feel secure in such a house? You won't. You'll need someone to keep you company all the time. That means you depend on them for your safety.

    What happens when you open up all the rooms, one by one, and let the light in? Now you know what's inside. Even if those rooms are filled with things you don't particularly like, you still feel more secure. That's the difference between security and insecurity, between self-reliance and between dependence. If we are feeling secure within, then we don't need to rely on anyone else for that security. That is the end of codependency.

- **What is the key to creating authentic, beautiful friendships?**

    Listen to the stories people tell you – not just through their words, but through their actions and their emotions – with your whole being. Which means we have to be earnest and present with others without any self-seeking or expectations. We have to allow them to fully express themselves. If their stories aren't that interesting to us, then how can we have that connection with them? When we are able to completely listen to others, without a desire to speak, validate, or criticize them, then we have begun to build that bridge to their subconscious mind. We have begun to create that deep fulfilling relationship with them.

    It doesn't matter even if we have never met them before, the connection can still be created. What's more, when you cultivate such a relationship with someone, it also begins to heal their wounds, without you doing anything about it. What's even more miraculous is that it begins to heal our wounds too. This happens because a true human connection is the deepest need any human being has. If this need is fulfilled, it instantly makes us whole. We feel heard, understood, secure and protected. Give yourself up to the present moment, and others will begin to feel that safety in your presence, and you in theirs.

- **Can you be happy and have no close relationships?**

    Sure, you can. We can always be self-reliant for our happiness. However, we can't find that specific kind of happiness that comes from being in a relationship, while being single. For instance, we can't feel what it is to be a parent without having a child, but we can certainly be happy without parenthood. It is just not the same kind of happiness.

So the real question is what kind of happiness does the seeker want, and what are they willing to give up to have it? If one wants the companionship of being with another person, then it's not possible to experience it without being in a relationship. That requires being vulnerable and facing the suffering that comes from both attachment and love.

Meditation

- **How does insight meditation work? Can you provide specific steps?**

    Insight meditation is to be practiced when one is in a place of calm, objective observation. To find that place, one has to have a practice of body-awareness meditation, based on focusing on one's breath, then sounds in one's surroundings, physical sensations and sights. This creates a strong inward connection and prepares one to look at one's thoughts. If body awareness is skipped, then thoughts can destabilize the mind and make observing impossible. It is like trying to observe a large river, while one is caught in its flow.

    In every meditation session, we can pick a problem and pass it through one of more of these questions:

    - What is the undercurrent of my thoughts saying right now?
        - » Why are they saying what they are saying?
          [For example, *"Because I am hurt."*]
        - » Why am I hurt? What exactly is hurt inside me?
        - » Where has this belief or attachment come from?
        - » Go deeper with each question, without rushing.
    - Which memory is surfacing more frequently?
    - What do my thoughts say about how I really feel?

Questions and Answers

- Can I look at my thoughts without calling them positive or negative?
- Can I redefine or better understand this particular emotion (e.g. jealousy, fear, pleasure, desire, pain?)
  - » Redefining something takes us deeper into it. (For instance, *'I am jealous'* becomes, *'I really wish she wasn't so happy.'*)
  - » This is usually a place where insights or breakthroughs happen.
- What is the real fear I have underneath this resistance?
- What is the hidden motive of my ego here? Am I deluding myself in any way?
  - » This is another place where an insight may present itself.
- Can I look at this insight in any different way or does this *feel* right?
  - » Develop a skill for sensing the correctness of your insights.
  - » An insight instantly creates energy and space in the mind.
  - » It feels good, even if it discovers a self-delusion or a mistake one has made.
- Am I rushing to conclusions or am I proceeding slowly and carefully?
  - » If you have any answer quickly, it's usually a wrong answer.
  - » Keep reminding yourself to slow down and take a step back.
- Have I ever reacted in a different way to the same situation before?
  - » This question is side-stepping our inquiry and re-entering it at a different point. This technique often reveals something we are refusing to see.

- What is *my* truth?
    » Avoid seeking security in comfortable answers.
    » Seek security in your *search and the ability to discover* your *personal* truths.

This inquiry creates a spontaneous flash of realization and suddenly takes us beyond the problem we are dealing with. If this examination gets overwhelming, it is always good to return to our centering practices (*breathing, seeing, feeling, hearing*) and taking a break. It is not necessary to push ourselves. If the mind is racing, it is time to step back. Insight meditation is a slow, deliberate and controlled observation of our past and present. It is an intense, yet ultimately an enjoyable practice. It slowly brings clarity and personal power back into our lives.

- **Isn't insight meditation, as you have described, just good old thinking?**

Far from it. Good old thinking is unconscious and uncontrolled flow of thoughts. It's our conditioning and the ego taking us on a ride. That's usual thinking. Insight meditation is a targeted unraveling of the problem. It's a conscious journey deeper into ourselves, where we are always in charge. Usual thinking is being lost; insight meditation allows us to begin exploring. However, in the end it does require thinking, just of a different quality.

- **Can you talk about your meditation practice?**

I started when I was ten years old by watching my father. He has meditated all his life. About 13 years ago, I started meditating a little more seriously. I read deeply into the works of J. Krishnamurti and Eckhart Tolle. Krishnamurti's teachings eventually began sending me into states of spontaneous meditation. This eventually became what I now call 'insight meditation,' a method that can neither be taught nor learned. It simply arises organically.

I usually meditate for 20 to 40 minutes at a time about four times a week. However, a few times every day, the eyes want to close and the mind surrenders and becomes still. It wants to find pockets of peace and I let it.

- **Being in the present feels boring. It's more interesting thinking about things. What am I doing wrong?**

    Nothing at all. At different points of time in our life, different things appeal to us. If silence isn't appealing, don't chase it just because someone says so. Keep it at the back of our mind that it's a place where one can heal from the past. When you find suffering, which you will at some point, this memory will arise from your subconscious mind and remind you of being present. And that will be enough.

- **How do I accept and let go of anxieties or physical wounds while regularly practicing to be better?**

    By consistently being able to find the present moment. The great irony about the present moment is that we can only *access* it, if we stop trying to *change* it (by accepting whatever is happening). The present is a place without problems; we get there when we stop trying to change what it contains. That means when we accept our anxiety, fear or even a physical injury fully, we are handed the key to rising above it. It's almost as if only those who accept their fate are somehow given the power to change it.

    When the conscious and subconscious mind give up the desire to change *what is* (even for a moment), we enter the present moment. Staying here for extended periods of time

Finding Awareness

rests the mind and automatically releases the past emotional burdens. You don't have to do anything. Just be still and let the healing begin. It is a natural process of life that happens only when we learn *how not to* reopen our wounds and just let them be.

- **How do you not let external things, mainly people's behavior, get into our minds and disturb our inner peace?**

  By deeply understanding that their behavior reflects their reality, not yours. As long as we keep associating our reality with their behavior, hurt is inevitable. When we are able to disconnect the two, then we can be present and deal with whatever they say or do. Understand your own triggers and study them. They are pointing to a whole new world within. Other people's behavior is an opportunity for us to understand ourselves better. If we get caught up in the superficial layers of anger, blame and resentment, then we have missed the opportunity to go inward. Instead, when we get triggered, asking ourselves, *"Why am I really angry?"* helps us go within. When we deeply understand what's happening, at all levels, we realize we are never angry at another person at all, even though that's what it seems like. We are only upset that we couldn't respond to the challenge they created for us. Deep down, we are angry at ourselves.

- **How do I address anxiety? It is nerve-wracking when I think about my future. How do you calm yourself in a situation where you are not able to control your mind or emotions?**

  Please note, we aren't referring to clinical anxiety. That may require professional help. We are talking about occasional fearful or anxious thoughts about our future or the general uncertainty in our lives. The solution to anxiety often is finding some sort of meditation practice. The correct practice is whichever works in making us feel calm and centered. This is one such practice.

Pay attention to your breathing. Observe how erratic it gets. Often just observing it makes it smooth and deep. Breathe about five to seven times per minute, and keep it going for 20 breaths. This will reset the mind. Our breath controls our heart rate, which regulates our feelings, which in turn regulates the emotional response and our thoughts. So if we can breathe right, we're more than halfway there. We're back in control. Then we can remain in the present moment, and wait for the correct response to arise.

With practice, this timeframe of five minutes to reset can be reduced to less than a few seconds. This means when we become aware that we are in the process of becoming angry, we can flip our breathing on like a switch and elicit a different response from the depth of our subconscious mind.

Try this 20-breaths meditation. This is a method to count to 20 without holding the actual numbers in your mind each time. As you take each breath, run your thumb down the index finger and count to four. Start with the tip of your finger and count the three grooves, to a total of four. Now you know how to get to 19. Go through all your fingers (16), and then use the index finger to count the tip and the grooves on the thumb (3). Then count one for the hand and you have a count of 20. Your mind can now focus on breathing, while your body goes through this almost wordless count.

Take these 20 conscious breaths with about five-second inhales and six-second exhales. Do this twice, for a total of 40 breaths. Anxiety cannot survive this meditation, because breathing evenly regulates the heart rate and clears the mind. Our emotions and thoughts begin to calm down and we find control.

- **Is it necessary to find a teacher if you are serious about spiritual growth?**

What is 'spirituality'? It's important to question that label because it instantly categorizes everything we know about ourselves. It's easy to say *"I am a spiritual person"* or *"I am a materialistic person."* You are essentially saying, *"I am this or that."* When we really question that label, there is no such thing as spirituality. What we call spirituality is acceptance of certain concepts given to us by those who call themselves spiritual, like a guru, whose purpose is to teach spirituality.

Let go of all those labels and look at your life as it is. Look at the fear, the confusion, the anxiety and the desires. Look at the self-doubt and the desire to follow someone. None of that is necessary when we are truly interested in having no internal conflict or fear. Then we can begin to look at ourselves as we are and understand what is happening. Then we can pick up a scientific book, as easily as a so-called spiritual book and simply learn about the world or ourselves.

Most of us don't want to be monks. We want to live among our friends and our family, while having a steady means of income without all the problems that come with this kind of living. In some ways it is harder to live in society and its myriad challenges, and still be free of the inward conflict it brings. So to be serious about one's *spiritual growth* is to learn how to live a *practical* life – a life of freedom, creativity, satisfaction and purpose.

Does any of this require a spiritual teacher? Perhaps not. One can examine one's own life, build a strong mental

Questions and Answers

model about how (one's own) life works and live by it. In that kind of a life, there is no dogma, arrogance, self-importance or confusion. You become your own teacher and student.

- **After months of meditation, I feel good but I'm not sure I'm doing it right? Can you give any tips?**

    This question usually arises when one has reached the second stage of meditation. Now, there are really *no stages* in this process, but to better understand it we can see meditation as having three stages. You can call them fundamental (centering practices), intermediate (insight meditation) and experienced (surrender practice).

    One is not better than the other; it is only more experienced than the other. Certainly a person in an experienced stage has no edge over a person who isn't, because experienced meditators spend most of their time practicing the fundamentals. When there are no problems to solve, they come back and rest in the body. Let's examine these three stages.

    The fundamental stage is when we cultivate a strong inner connection with our body. Centering meditations, yoga, martial arts, tai chi or any other types of physical exercises can allow us to complete this stage. The common factor is that one is able to stay with physical sensations for long periods of time. One is able to feel comfortable with oneself. If not, the next stage *shouldn't* be entered. It may only increase our inner confusion. So some of us, who have trauma often have to spend a long time in this stage of meditation and that's okay. We begin to feel a slight frustration because we haven't solved any big problems in our life yet. The key to those problems is the next stage. Assuming one is able to stay centered for perhaps fifteen to forty minutes at a time, we can begin practicing Insight meditation.

This second stage addresses our conditioning, our thoughts or emotions. It develops our ability to hold a problem gently in our conscious awareness and peel it layer by layer. We uncover the true nature of our inner reality until there is an insight and the conflict between our thoughts comes to an end. This brings a release of mental energy and instant change in our lives.

The experienced stage begins when we reach the limits of insight meditation and welcome the idea of letting go and surrender. We are occasionally able to see a particular situation without trying to change it, or judge it. We are able to live effortlessly and flow with a given moment. We feel emotionally secure and are able to feel states of deep silence and rest. We begin to open up to our calling or purpose.

- **I feel like I've been in a cocoon, isolating and concentrating on my inner growth. Am I escaping life?**

   Solitude is a necessary condition for deep inner work. This is why some meditation retreats require stopping all contact with the outside world. They want the meditator to go deep into themselves. Only when we are alone can we really face ourselves. This solitude is the space where we can create something new. It is the only place where we can discover who we are, without the influence of society. However, this is a temporary phase which ends once we find greater control and harmony within. Then we can re-engage with society with more power. During this process some painful relationships may end, others may be transformed. Yet our connection to other human beings is ultimately a core need, which we all eventually return to.

- **All meditation teachers say letting go is key. What does *"letting go of thoughts"* really mean?**

    We can't let go of thoughts, because the ego, *"I"* is also a thought. So when we try to let go of thinking, we need a thought to clear away the rest of them. That one thought, which is a central actor, is the *me-thought*. Think of it like using a blowtorch to extinguish a fire. We just create more fire. Thoughts leave when the conflict between them is resolved. For instance, we ask *"Should I take this job or shouldn't I?"* These opposing thoughts are trying to solve a problem and when that solution is found, both of them disappear and leave behind silence.

    What is often referred to as letting go, is not of the thoughts, but *the desire to solve* the problems they are creating. That points to surrendering to the present state and giving into the things we are unable to change. If that is what they mean by letting go, then it is indeed the key to everything.

Surrender

- **How do you accept something?**

    By examining how resisting it is causing pain. We can observe how our natural reaction to resist something creates suffering. We can see how it's making us afraid, confused and exhausted. Then we ask ourselves if we want to keep carrying on with it for the rest of our lives. Resistance gets us stuck, while acceptance teaches us how to flow with life. When we understand this, we accept. There is nothing to do, except understand. The doing happens on its own. It's like realizing that a snake in front of us is poisonous. We don't have to *try* and stay away from it. We naturally do! If we are forcing ourselves to accept, that just means we don't yet understand why acceptance is the way forward. That is okay. When the right time comes, we do.

- **What's the difference between accepting and surrendering?**

Accepting is not complete surrender. Acceptance is simply the opposite of resistance. As resistance is decreasing, acceptance is increasing. When all resistance is gone, so is all acceptance. It exists only as a counter to resistance.

When the battle of opposites is over, we have found surrender. In the state of surrender, it becomes impossible to call something good or bad. There are no judgments anymore. In the state of acceptance, we may still have judgments. For instance, we may accept our fear and yet think the fear should leave us. We may still fight with our fear, pretend courage, while accepting the fear exists. However, with surrender, there is no fighting back, for there is nothing *wrong* with fear. It can stay as long as it pleases. It can grow and consume us, and that is okay too. It is not up to us anymore what happens next. The ego's relationship with its belongings is transformed. It has no desire to change anything.

What we fight becomes stronger.

What we accept becomes weaker.

And what we surrender to becomes the reason for our transformation.

- **If I make peace with the present moment, does that mean I will never change?**

    Accepting something for the moment doesn't mean being stuck with it forever. In fact, when we truly accept something, the thing we accepted instantly begins to transform itself. Why? Because accepting something ends our inner conflict with it. Our relationship with it has already changed. We have become a different person – a person who is not caught up in inner conflict. This means we are no longer wasting psychological energy on it. That mental energy now becomes available. It is felt in the form of an idea or an intuition to act. That action weakens or dissolves the problem we were resisting. Come to think of it, that was the transformation we had been waiting for. It came not from continuous resistance, but occasional acceptance and moving with the problem.

- **How can I learn to embrace change without losing my "fight?"**

    The answer is by surrendering to change. Surrendering is not really losing the "fight" with progress; it's losing the fight with oneself, therefore, it opens the door to progress. We give up resisting the emotional burdens which are draining our energy. We put them down and walk free. The energy we save in the process can now be used to formulate solutions that further our growth.

    The fear of losing one's drive is based on an incorrect understanding of how surrender works. Surrender doesn't make your drive weaker; it clarifies it and makes it immensely powerful. Surrender does to your drive, what fire does to steel. It tempers your will and makes it stronger. It takes away all the roadblocks in your path so you see farther than

Finding Awareness

you ever have. It unlocks your real potential. When you surrender, your true nature begins to show itself to you. Your deepest calling steps forward and begins to guide you. Instead of hearing the chaotic chatter of the ego, you hear the calm voice of your intuition. It leads you out of dark places and brings you into light and clarity.

- **How can I be okay with letting go of something I deeply want?**

   By experimenting with it. See what happens when you truly let go and don't expect anything from a person or a situation. Once we understand the principle behind it, it starts becoming easier. Eventually it becomes a natural way of being. As we practice letting go more and more, our mind begins to feel the contrast between the pain of craving and peace that comes from letting go. This newly learned skill teaches the mind how to transform itself. To let go is to say, *"I am okay if this doesn't work out the way I want it to"* and yet feel nothing but peace. It frees us from both the attachment to success and the fear of failure in a single act.

- **How to find flow in life?**

   Flow is found at the edge of effort and surrender. We are conditioned to try harder when things get difficult. When things are hard, it's time to step back from the constant pushing towards our objective. It's time to take a moment of rest. When we consciously walk away from the conditioned desire to struggle and push harder, we create a vacuum or space in our minds. This space can't remain there for long. It gets filled by our intuition. When we consciously abandon effort this space is born. It is full of possibilities. From its fertile soil creative ideas emerge. Intuition comes alive in it.

If effort is the tool of our conscious mind, intuition is the tool of our subconscious mind. Working with this state of intuition is *flow*. It is found at the edge of effort and surrender, as we begin to let go of one and enter the other.

- **How do I identify when to act and work, versus when to surrender and receive?**

    Surrender until it's time to act, and act until it's time to surrender. There is a continuous flow between the two. Like the yin-yang symbol, they both move together. When a task isn't going in the direction we want it to, we take a break, we let go and surrender. Now, we get clues on how to proceed and we act on those. If we get stuck again, we repeat the cycle. This idea usually creates confusion when our goals are practical in nature.

    For example: finding a job, completing a work project, running a marathon, competing in sports or preparing for an exam. For these goals, we can use affirmations, meticulous planning, visualizations or positive thinking. Using whatever we need in order to proceed. Since these goals do not involve our unresolved subconscious past, they respond to our effort and willpower.

    However, if we are working on goals which require creativity, interpersonal dynamics or reconditioning of the ego, start with surrender. (For example: improving a relationship, getting over a relationship, forgiving oneself, rising above hurt, letting go of an addiction or getting over a deep-seated fear.) Here we can't use affirmations or willpower since these goals deal with our unresolved past. Any effort or forcing backfires, and creates more suffering.

    Knowing when to surrender and when to act is a skill. The only way to train it, is to begin.

- **How do you balance surrendering to 'what is' with being assertive/standing up for yourself?**

    Surrender is an internal act of ending the battle with our past, which is unchangeable. It is not about surrendering to another human being. If someone violates our trust, attacks, bullies or abuses us, we have to stand up for ourselves. However, here too if we are present and listening, our response to them is appropriate. It protects us as well as them from undue harm.

    The state of surrender is not to accept defeat from our challenges; it is to take away the resistance that prevents us from responding fully to them. This total response to a challenge tends to have a natural and organic assertiveness. When we have surrendered, we are also listening deeply. Such listening ensures that we are connected to ourselves during any unpleasant interaction. So when we speak up, our response is fearless and clear. We never let fear or anger take root in our conscious mind. As a result, a surrendered state of mind results in complete action, which is to respond appropriately to any given challenge. A surrendered mind isn't caught up in self-protection, therefore it can act fearlessly. Any mind that speaks and acts fearlessly naturally stands up for itself, without even knowing that it did so.

- **How do I stay calm during the never ending storm of suffering?**

    By learning how to surrender to suffering. Our suffering is never a problem. Our resistance to it is. Suffering is an inseparable part of life. Even if we don't have any attachments, we suffer because of love. Suffering is unavoidable and, as such, it shouldn't be avoided. If we do, we become cold and callous. Our heart becomes closed and impenetrable like a rock. That is no way to live.

When we refuse to resist suffering, it comes and goes as it pleases. Then we become softened by it. It teaches us how to love others and how to be compassionate and caring human beings, for we know what it means to suffer. When we stop resisting our pain, it no longer feels as painful. Life feels calm even in the depth of suffering. This is the key to going beyond suffering, addictions, fear and almost everything – to flow with life and becoming one with it. Then nothing needs to change and, therefore, everything does.

- **I am afraid of losing control. How do I let go of control?**

    Losing control is a fear that is borne out of the persistent desire to hold on to something we think of as security. Total control is impossible; so is total security. Why hold on at all? Allow yourself to feel whatever you feel, apart from, of course, physically harming yourself or someone else. If you feel that, please consult a therapist.

    Otherwise, let it all happen, for it's happening anyway. You are barely able to hold on for a semblance of control and are miserable because of it. If you let go, you'll see something interesting happen. The more willingly you give up control, the more control is given back to you. The less you grasp, the more you hold. Your fate is like water; you can't close your palm if you must hold. You have to be gentle. The fighting and grasping creates this fear of losing control. Don't resist. Surrender. Let go.

    You think you're hanging off a low branch and are worried about it snapping, then falling into an abyss. Just let go and see what happens. You'll land on earth, covered in soft grass, just two inches below your feet. Then you can walk away and be free of all those problems you have created for yourself.

Finding Awareness

- **I am afraid of returning to my low point if I surrender. How do I prevent it from happening?**

    Once we make some progress – with our fears, our addictions or relationships – we are always nervous about ending up where we started. If this fear exists, it often means that our transition to our new selves is not yet permanent. That is okay. These patterns are so powerful that they often take years to fully transform. The key is to not fight the resurgence of that low point. Instead, you say: *"If I go down again, so be it. I will be aware when it happens and see how it happens. Then I will start again from zero."* This act of allowing our fear to arise and exit is a powerful way to invite change. This is the way of surrender. At some point our mind just drops it and moves on. If we dread that regression, the fear builds up because of our resistance to it, and we end up creating what we fear. Instead, if we assist and surrender to it, it begins to arise and fade away.

Ego

- **Can you explain the difference between ego and self-respect?**

    Self-respect accounts for other people; the ego doesn't. The ego is concerned with 'who' is right and self-respect with 'what' is right. The ego is primarily concerned with words like me, mine and myself. Self-respect may not prioritize, but it certainly accounts for 'you, yours and yourself,' along with one's own priorities. The ego is always feeling threatened and protecting itself. It is fundamentally insecure. Self-respect is secure. The only time self-respect protects us is when it knows what is happening to us is wrong. For example, such a thing as verbal, emotional or physical abuse is wrong no matter who it happens to. There is no ego associated with calling abuse wrong. It is not an egoic judgment. That's why self-respect knows when to walk away from a relationship. The ego is confused and continues to suffer because of the attachments it has. Our ego is present from the beginning, but our self-respect grows as we understand our egos and go beyond them. Ego creates conflict easily; self respect helps resolve that conflict.

- **How do I get my ego to stop dominating my thoughts and actions?**

    You can't. That's what the ego does. What you can do is observe the ego and learn its ways. The more you (the ego) become aware of it, the less it can do what it wants to do. You don't have to force anything either way. Change in the ego, by definition, happens without willful effort or direction. If there is a direction or power of will, then that direction is a creation of the ego. When ego tries to change itself, it gets wrapped up, like a snake trying to eat its own tail. It may bring about superficial changes, but fundamentally, it's still the ego.

    When our self-awareness exposes our egoic behaviors, they begin to dissolve on their own. There is no action, except accurate and judgment-free observation. This way is quite simple in that sense. It has no elaborate steps. For example, if we catch ourselves becoming angry, it feels absurd to continue to go ahead and feel angry anyway. Forced anger is no longer anger. We walk away from it. We depart from an unconscious behavior of the ego, simply because we became aware of it. More accurately, the ego can't go on acting blindly. It unravels itself the more it practices self-awareness.

The more self-awareness takes over, the more the ego dissolves itself.

- **It seems like the ego is our enemy. How to kill our ego?**

Why do we want to end the ego? There are two main reasons. First one is so that we can become someone superior to the ego. The higher self, the universal consciousness, the enlightened one and so on. Doesn't that sound more like another trick of the ego trying to make itself look better? Trying to be enlightened or awakened seems like a clever delusion of the ego. Is our ego not chasing another special experience? Some egos chase the experience of being a billionaire, while some the experience of enlightenment. How are they any different? From the ego's point of view they are both the same – a pleasurable experience. This is a hard truth to face for most of us because of the refuge it offers, but it's a truth we must confront head on.

This brings us to the second reason why we want to end the ego. In order to end our suffering. Then the question arises, who is it trying to end the ego anyway, if not the ego itself? Can the ego ever end itself, or does the very act of trying to end itself perpetuate it? A different way of asking the same question is, can you ever create silence by talking about it? Or can fire ever extinguish fire? The answer is clear.

The ego is not the enemy. If we consider it to be as such and try to get rid of it, we supplant it with another version of ourselves as the 'egoless me.' This egoless self is a figment of our imagination. It is an ideal which we want to reach, not a present reality. So it only creates more conflict with what's real. Yet the idea is so alluring that it gives our ego an opportunity to put on some lipstick and refuse to recognize itself in the mirror. The higher self, afterall, may be nothing but the lower self in disguise. The 'me' can't dissolve the 'me'; it can only make more of itself.

The only way to deal with this conundrum is to simply watch the ego play its tricks. That is to constantly learn about our unconscious behaviors. The ego is therefore our teacher, who we learn from by watching and listening. It may not be our friend, but it certainly isn't our enemy.

- **The more I observe my ego, the more it seems to become louder. Is this true?**

  This can happen for two reasons. One, since we are becoming more sensitive, we see more of the ego than we did before. Two, we are resisting what we see. For instance, when we see ourselves being selfish, we criticize and judge ourselves for being so. When we criticize ourselves, we have stopped taking note of what else our ego is up to. Furthermore, whatever we attack directly becomes stronger if its source is our unresolved past. So it feels as if the ego is becoming louder, or the old patterns are becoming more deeply rooted.

  Instead of judging ourselves, noticing that the ego is selfish, making a mental note of it, then moving on is a much better approach. This lets us be okay with who we are at the moment. That mental note we make sinks deep in the subconscious mind over time and we begin to notice more and more of the same patterns of pettiness, selfishness, conceit and deception. Learning about the ego is an exercise in being wrong. Self-awareness dissolves our ego from the inside out, by repeatedly revealing its shortcomings. Yet, all these apparent shortcomings are only to be noticed and put aside. There is nothing to be done. Soon, corrective actions begin to happen on their own. We can't act with pettiness if we know we are being small-minded. We can't be jealous when we realize how absurd jealousy is when we love the people we are jealous of. As a result, we eventually end up doing the right thing. We change without trying to. We transform, effortlessly.

- **A lot of people say,** *"You are not your thoughts. You are awareness."* **Is this true?**

Being the observer of your thoughts is to be separate from the stream of your thoughts. So when you say, *"I am aware of my thoughts. I am watching them,"* you are that observer. This is quite straightforward.

Now, who is this observer watching the thoughts? It is the ego, right? Who else can it be? It is you, the ego, who is observing its own thoughts. So, the one who says, *"I am aware"* is just a thought, which is separated from the other thoughts. It is the ego, the me-thought. Self-awareness is the ego watching other thoughts, emotions, memories, etc. The ego is constantly watching and judging itself. It says, *"Fear, you need to go away from my life"* or *"Pleasure, I need more of you."* These judgments are simply more thoughts. Even when one is aware, the ego is manipulating its belongings (fears, anxieties, addictions, memories, etc.). This is a better state than being completely unaware of ego's activities, but it is still the ego.

But what happens when during this practice of self-awareness, the ego reaches the point of surrender. When it feels absurd to judge its own actions, when it can look at its fear quietly, without saying a word? Where the me-thought becomes inactive, the dark side of the ego, merges with its light side. The ego becomes one complete whole. It has become integrated. One becomes a total human being, with no desire to change anything about oneself.

Even if this happens for one second, in that time, the ego and its belongings merge into one. The splintered mind comes together to become complete. Then, and only then, is there pure awareness. One can no longer say, *"Your true nature is awareness"* for there is no '*you*' in there. So then what is one's true nature?

One's true nature is obviously the ego! Because that's the *only reality* accessible to us at this moment. Everything else is a self-comforting supposition. It takes us further away, and not closer to ourselves.

- **How do you know if a decision is ego-based or understanding-based?**

  A decision borne out of self-centered thinking always creates inward conflict. This is so because the self is very small compared to the vastness of life. When it wants to expand itself and control the 'winds,' it fails miserably. The ego is already in conflict with other egos and with the world. Anything it does for itself creates more conflict . One has to be very sensitive to observe this in one's daily life.

  Understanding, on the other hand, is based on the situation, not on the self. The actual situation is independent of the ego. Understanding asks, *"What is right?"* not *"Who is right?"* Therefore, it fits into the scheme of things. It's based on the situation and insights or facts, not on opinions or beliefs. That's why it creates clarity, peace and calmness. It resolves inner and outer conflict. If you feel inner turmoil, that's an egoic decision, if you feel peace, even if things didn't turn out the way you wanted, that's an understanding-based decision. One needs to develop a feel for it.

  Understanding-based decisions don't create regret or chaos in the mind. For example, purchasing something expensive

Finding Awareness

on a whim gives us a temporary high, then creates doubt and regret. However, purchasing it when the time is right gives us lasting satisfaction. Some questions to lead us towards understanding.

- "Do I really need this right now?"
- "Does this feel right?"
- "Is this a kind and compassionate thing to do?"
- "Do I believe this is good for my mental peace in the long run?"
- "Is this short-term pleasure worth the long-term problems it might cause?"
- "Is getting back at them going to really make me happy?"
- "Is this who I really am?"

- **What are your views about nirvana and enlightenment?**

    I believe it's a waste of time to chase enlightenment, because even if it did exist, it surely wouldn't come to a person just because they desired it. Unless it was an endurance goal like winning an Olympic gold medal, enlightenment wouldn't be a thing you chase and achieve. So, either enlightenment is quite a material objective like winning first prize in a competition, or it's something spiritual, which would defy predictability and effort. If it's the former, it's an egoistic movement (not negative or positive, just something that follows the rules of will-power and effort), and if the latter it would refute the laws of cause and effect humans love to cling to. Pick one; you can't pick both. Logically thinking, even by using the existing definitions of that word, it seems like a false target to chase.

    Yet another problem is that of seeking an experience someone else has described. We read about other people's experiences and feel how marvelous it must be to be enlightened. Then we pretend to have it when we feel warmth in the spine or chakras etc., believing we must be ascending towards God. It all becomes quite childish once we really see what we (our ego) have been up to. We don't know what enlightenment must feel like, so we estimate what it must be, based on the descriptions we read, and chase that experience however we can. In the meanwhile, the same people who chase enlightenment also define it as an experience that *"ends all desires."* How can we hope to end all desires by desiring to be enlightened?

These two conflicts, when understood deeply, end the trouble that this unnecessary word creates.

- **Why am I so attached to the past and what *could have been*?**

    The subconscious mind never thinks the past is over. It believes that it can be changed and is trying to do so all the time. This is why we reminisce about the *could haves* and *should have beens*. We remember those memories and modify them slightly each time we recall them. If we closely observe our recollections, we notice this slight and *deliberate* modification. We replay our memories and interactions over and over with subtle changes. If we wonder what it would have been to still be in a relationship with someone, we imagine being married to them, or saying things to them we never actually did. These thoughts are a result of our subconscious mind attempting to change the past. The conscious mind can and does accept the past is finished. The subconscious mind has no such *"illusions"*. When we become more aware of this deep form of resistance to the past we may have a sudden insight about how strange it is to try and change what has already happened, especially givenhow much pain it created. Then we will drop it like a hot piece of coal. The attachment instantly falls away.

- **How do I detach myself from my possessions and the people I am attached to?**

    The opposite of attachment isn't detachment. It is freedom. An attachment falls away naturally when the mind sees the role that attachment plays in creating suffering. When we see the silliness of how a scratch on our new car, or a coffee stain on our dress makes us upset, it stops happening. When we see how we think of ourselves as having various identities based on being a doctor, a musician, a meditator, a writer etc., or how we suffer because of our attachment-born expectations from others, those attachments dissolve. An attachment begins with receiving (false) security from an object, idea or a person, and ends with those things becoming a part of our identity. The deeper we look, the more attachments we find. The more we understand how every single one of them makes us suffer, the more they fall away.

- **How to get what we want without getting attached to it?**

    By asking ourselves, *"Am I okay with not getting this? Am I okay with falling?"* If the answer is a genuine *yes*, then we can do whatever is necessary to move towards that goal. If we are not okay with failure, then we're still attached to the goal, and that's alright. All it means is that some form of suffering, arising from that goal, is inevitable.

    Please note, there is no right or wrong in either of the approaches, because suffering is fundamental to human life. There is nothing inherently wrong with suffering. A lot of people are willing to greatly suffer for their objectives. They are willing to make hard sacrifices. For instance, a world-class athlete can't win an Olympic gold medal without being fully attached to her goal. That's her path. She is willing to suffer, if she fails. We all have to choose our paths carefully and be at peace with what we choose. The only thing to remember is where there is attachment, there will also be some form of suffering. They go together.

If we want to achieve a goal without suffering because of it, then the only path forward is to be okay with failure, which is surrendering to all outcomes and being at peace with whatever happens. Then there is freedom, and a different kind of inspiration. A kind that is unconditional, and therefore can't be affected by changing life situations. From there, the journey becomes enjoyable and we can hope to arrive at the end of it without destroying ourselves in the process, or the world.

Goals

- **What's the purpose of life and how do I find my life's purpose?**

  The purpose of life itself is to keep us alive. That's all. What the purpose of an individual's life is for them to find out. It doesn't have to be anything glorious, only authentic. One can use this simple guideline to figure out their purpose.

  We have to start with our drifts, things which we naturally like doing. If we don't know what we like, then it's time to explore. We can undertake this exploration by being more curious about the world around us by talking to people who we find interesting, exploring art forms or reading books about the subjects we like. But most of all, we just have to look far back into our past and examine the things which pull us toward them.

Let's assume for the sake of this discussion, there are four such things we discover. Now we can narrow things down by asking, how many of those do we enjoy doing so much that we lose track of time? How many of these four do we seem to have a natural ability for? Maybe three things remain. These are the things we *love* doing. Out of these three, how many are such that we also lose our sense of self, while doing them? That is, we feel we are involved with something greater than our limited egos? We get such deep satisfaction from these activities that we are willing to face opposition from friends or family in order to do them. Maybe two activities remain, these are our passions. To our passions, we ask the most important question there is to ask. Do I feel as if I am responsible for doing this particular thing in the world? Responsible not to someone else, but to myself. Do I believe in a unique way that it should be done? And do I feel as if I have no choice in the matter, even though no one else is pressuring me? If the answer to all three is *yes*, then the thing that remains is our purpose.

- Do I deeply enjoy doing it?
- Do I lose track of time while doing it?
- Do I have a natural ability for it?
- Do I feel as if something greater than me is involved?
- Can I stand against opposition in order to do it?
- Do I have a unique vision about it?
- Do I feel as if I have no choice in the matter?

If all these conditions are met, we have discovered our purpose.

Such a thing could even be being the best father, mother or provider there is. It doesn't have to be anything glorious, it only has to be true to our deepest self. Notice how the consideration of impact, money, power or fame are totally irrelevant when we look for our purpose. A purpose is something that gives us meaning in life. Sometimes, it is to take care of a sick child, or an aging parent. At other times, it is to sing, write or create. Finding your purpose is an intensely personal and a beautiful journey. Let no one else take it for you.

- **How do you build focus and motivation to do something you love?**

  Set a time of day to do it then do it in spite of the odds you face. Soon, you'll build momentum and a process will lay itself out. Discipline is important, but it can't be forced. It has to exist easily. This *easy discipline* happens when we build a process around the thing which we love doing. For instance, if we want to start a business, then getting up early to think, plan and work on our ideas takes discipline. However, creatively approaching the problems we face on a daily basis, while developing that business requires calmness, focus, ease and intuition. Understanding the difference between when to *control* something and when to *surrender*, then using the two wisely is important. It helps us deepen and strengthen our creative process and creates focus and motivation as we see the rapid progress we make.

  Motivation is also a product of clarity and vision. Clarify how exactly you want your work to look and sharpen your vision. How should it be different and unique? What are things that anger or move you? What are the things which you will never compromise on? If you are willing to do anything to get ahead, then you don't have a passion for your work, but for the end result, which may be money, power, fame, etc. But if you won't do anything that violates

Finding Awareness

your principles and your vision, then you are in love with the process. It means you won't stop when you taste success once. You will keep following your process. You'll keep going.

So, what is the core reason why you want to do something? Meditate on that core reason and embody it at all times. That reason will become a source of inspiration not just you, but even those around you.

- **How can I be more patient when waiting for some things, such as love, a fulfilling career, etc.?**

  Spend less time pondering your future and more time doing more of what you enjoy doing and engaging in things which support your growth and creative satisfaction. It could be pursuing a hobby, working on a project or giving back to the community. This repeated act of doing things which we love creates what can be called a *process-orientation*. We begin to enjoy the process more with each passing day. It makes us more patient and we can now wait longer to find success, while constantly making progress. This helps build ourselves to the point where we see more opportunities, engage differently with the world, become less afraid and more confident in trying new things. As you align with your drifts and enjoy life more and more, the things which you want now begin to appear within reach. They never left their spot and came to you because of some hidden law, but you moved towards those things naturally by following your own path.

- **What motivates you to write?**

  People who deeply suffer. In other words, ordinary people facing extraordinary odds. Those who stare death in the face and do not flinch. That is what inspires me – a human being's ability to gracefully face their own end. When I write, I am addressing human suffering, the thread that connects us all. Death and suffering are very close to me when I write, not thoughts of physical harm, but an undercurrent of the finality and the truth they capture. To find inspiration in death, one has to look far beyond the depression and fear it invokes. It reveals the meaning of what it means to live. It infuses each waking moment with love, compassion and inspiration.

Endnote References

Chapter 3

- *"Research done on non-human primates"* - https://www.nature.com/articles/nature01963

Chapter 6

- *"plunges us into the depths of emotional isolation too"* - Life after trauma: personality and daily life experiences of traumatized people, https://pubmed.ncbi.nlm. nih.gov/7782991/

Chapter 7

- *"various neurotransmitters and hormones in our body are balanced"* - Stress, neurotransmitters, corticosterone and body-brain integration, https://pubmed.ncbi.nlm.nih.gov/ 22285436/

Chapter 14

- *"He looked down towards his feet"* - Alex did make history that day becoming the first human to free-solo Half Dome in Yosemite. You can

Endnote References

find plenty of images of him on the "Thank God ledge" on the worldwide web.

- *"Heart rate and shortness of breath"* - Increased heartbeat-evoked potential during REM sleep in nightmare disorder, https://pubmed.ncbi.nlm.nih.gov/30739843/

Chapter 15

- *"our breathing is shallow, rapid and uneven"* - Breathing rhythms and emotions, https://pubmed.ncbi.nlm.nih.gov/18487316/
- *"because we are the most relaxed we can be"* - Emotions and respiratory patterns: review and critical analysis, , https://pubmed.ncbi.nlm.nih.gov/7995774/
- *"create emotions that match those patterns"* - Respiratory feedback in the generation of emotion, https://www.researchgate.net/publication/232965660
- *"the more it regulates our heart rate"* - How heart rate variability affects emotion regulation brain networks, http://ncbi.nlm.nih.gov/pmc/articles/PMC5761738
- *"when our heart rate and breathing synchronize"* - Resonance Frequency breathing, https://www.ncbi.nlm.nih.gov/pmc/articles/PMC5575449/
- *"diaphragmatic breathing"* - The Effect of Diaphragmatic Breathing on Attention, Negative Affect and Stress in Healthy Adults, https://www.ncbi.nlm.nih.gov/pmc/articles/PMC5455070/

Chapter 21

- *"positive and beneficial core beliefs"* - Adult attachment styles and core beliefs, are they linked? https://onlinelibrary.wiley.com/doi/abs/10.1002/cpp.345
- *"takes root in our minds"* - Adult attachment, parenting experiences, and core beliefs about self and others. https://www.sciencedirect.com/science/article/abs/pii/S0191886907004254

297

Printed in Great Britain
by Amazon